D1431661

MICHIGAN BUSINESS PAPERS

Number 62

The Department of Economics at Western Michigan University is pleased to cooperate with the Division of Research at the Graduate School of Business Administration, The University of Michigan, in presenting this collection of papers in which five distinguished authorities explore various implications of the current levels and distribution of the world's supply of food and energy sources. This volume is the eleventh in a series published under these auspices.

MICHIGAN BUSINESS
PAPERS   Number 62

The Political Economy of Food and Energy

*Lectures given at Western Michigan University
under the sponsorship of the Department of
Economics, academic year 1975–76*

Edited by

LOUIS JUNKER

A publication of the
Division of Research
Graduate School of Business Administration
University of Michigan
Ann Arbor

ISBN-0-87712-177-x

Copyright © 1977
by
The University of Michigan

All rights reserved
Printed in the United States of America

HD
9000.6
. P65
1977

7857

To Frances, Nanette,
Louis and James

ACKNOWLEDGMENTS

In a venture such as this there are always credits that are cumulated and therefore debts that need to be gratefully acknowledged. Western Michigan University has supported the Economics Lecture Series for twelve years and thanks must go to Dean Cornelius Loew and to Associate Dean Tilman Cothran for support of this year's lectures, the eleventh set in the series.

Special appreciation must go to Dr. Raymond Zelder, Chairman of the Economics Department, for giving unfailingly of his time and efforts to help make this a successful lecture series and published volume. Although he may disagree with much that is published in this volume, he nevertheless spared no effort to make the lecturers welcome on our campus.

Grateful appreciation for technical and professional advice and assistance must go to the members of this year's lecture series committee, Professor Jared Wend and Professor Wayland Gardner.

How is it possible for the editor to properly thank those efficient and good-humored departmental secretaries who so often brought order out of chaos in the arrangement and organization of the myriad of details involved in presenting such a program? This acknowledgment of my indebtedness to Cress Strand and Christine Truckey is but a small downpayment on the great service they have rendered. In addition graduate students Steve Cortese and Glenn Paiva performed necessary and important services in helping to tape the talks of each speaker as they were delivered, from which tapes the first drafts of these published articles were drawn.

Of course, no volume such as this one can possibly be published without the crucial work of skilled editors. Mrs. Henrietta Slote and Miss Alice Preketes of the Division of Research, Graduate School of Business Administration, University of Michigan, performed these editorial tasks with consummate skill as well as with a light touch, and for this they have my thanks and respect.

My greatest debt is reserved for the authors of the papers in this volume. Not only did they make a great effort to present their ideas interestingly, they also did so with great professional skill and knowledge. These authors display an all-too-rare scholarly persistence for trying to see the subject matter of their particular concern in ever-widening scope and detail. They offer hope and guidance to the "disciplinarians" who may be struggling to form a transdiciplinarian approach to the persistent social problems of our times. I am grateful for their knowledge and intellectual guidance as well as for their friendship, which I cherish.

Last, but certainly not least, I would like to thank my colleagues, as a body, in the Department of Economics. Aside from those rarer moments of internecine strife that have occurred in our Department from time to time they have nevertheless allowed me to practice my unorthodox and radical arts in their midst and have been generous in their provision of a great deal of latitude, not only in the courses that I teach but in the constitution of this seminar and volume. For these opportunities I remain in their debt.

L.J.

Western Michigan University
Kalamazoo, Michigan
November, 1976

CONTENTS

TABLES

FIGURES

ABOUT THE CONTRIBUTORS

GEORGE BORGSTROM *is professor of Food Sciences at Michigan State University. An internationally recognized authority on the role of fish protein in world feeding, Professor Borgstrom was awarded the Institute of Food Technologists International award in 1975; in 1974 he received the Wahlberg Gold Medal from the Royal Swedish Society of Anthropology and Geography. Professor Borgstrom has lectured widely on world food resources and population and has served as consultant and adviser in many countries, both poor and developed. Among his extensive writings are:* Too Many: A Study of the Earth's Biological Limitations; The Hungry Planet: The Modern World at the Edge of Famine; World Food Resources; Focal Points: A Global Food Strategy, *and* The Food and People Dilemma.

MICHAEL PERELMAN *is assistant professor of Economics at the University of California at Chico. He is a graduate of the University of Michigan, where he took his B.A. in Economics, and he holds the Ph.D. degree in Agricultural Economics from the University of California at Berkeley. Dr. Perelman's testimony on "Efficiency and Agriculture" before the U.S. Senate's Committee on Migratory Labor appears in part 3A of* Farmworkers in Rural America, 1971-72. *He is the author of many articles in economic analysis and in agricultural economics. His forthcoming book,* The Myth of Agricultural Efficiency, *should prove to be a valuable addition to the debate on this subject.*

RUSSELL PARKER *is presently at the University of Wisconsin on leave from his post as Assistant to the Director of the Bureau of Economics of the Federal Trade Commission, a position he has held for five years. Dr. Parker took his Ph.D. in Economics from the University of Wisconsin in 1962. He has taught at Wisconsin, Michigan State University, and at the U.S. Department of Agriculture Graduate School. His work has ranged from industry studies to analyses of structural trends in U.S. industry, structure-performance relationships, and corporate mergers. Recently he has contributed actively to investigations of the food industry about which he has written for the F.T.C. Dr. Parker in 1968 and 1969 served as senior staff of the Cabinet Committee on Price Stability, a special staff of the President's Council of Economic Advisers. He is the major author of influential economic reports including* Economic Report on Corporate Mergers *and* Industrial Structure and Competitive Policy.

HERBERT I. SCHILLER *is a major contributor to the study of communication. He is trained in both Economics and Communications and he is at present Professor of Communications at the Third College of the University of California at San Diego. In recent years he has served as Visiting Professor in many countries, including the Netherlands, Finland, Sweden, and Israel, and from 1966 to 1970 he was Research Professor and editor of the* Quarterly Review of Economics and Business *at the University of Illinois. Since completing his Ph.D. at New York University in 1960, Professor Schiller has written extensively. His book* Mass Communication and the American Empire *has, for many, achieved the status of a classic, and his* The Mind Managers *is a following study. Most recently Professor Schiller has published* Communication and Cultural Domination.

NICHOLAS GEORGESCU-ROEGEN *has recently retired from Vanderbilt University, where he held the posts of Professor of Economics from 1949 to 1969 and Distinguished Professor of Economics from 1969 to 1976. He is at present Visiting Professor at the University of West Virginia. Known as one of the most innovative thinkers in the profession, Dr. Georgescu-Roegen has received many honors which reflect his colleagues' admiration. He has been elected Distinguished Fellow of the American Eco-*

nomics Association (1971) and Fellow of the American Academy of Arts and Sciences (1973), and he held the Richard T. Ely Lectureship of the A.E.A. in 1969.

Professor Georgescu-Roegen completed his M.A. in Mathematics at the University of Bucharest in 1926 and his Doctorate in Statistics at the University of Paris in 1930. He pursued post-doctoral research under Karl Pearson at University College, London, from 1930 to 1932. In 1948 and 1949 he served as Lecturer and Research Associate at Harvard University. He has been a Visiting Professor in Japan and Brazil.

Among his diverse and distinguished publications are: Analytical Economics: Issues and Problems, *and* The Entropy Law and the Economic Process *(Harvard University Press, 1966 and 1971 respectively). New books by Professor Georgescu-Roegen are soon to be released by Princeton University Press and Allanheld, Osmun & Company.*

LOUIS JUNKER *is Professor of Economics at Western Michigan University in Kalamazoo, Michigan. He is a specialist in the area of institutional-radical economic theory, economic development and the political economy of food and nutrition. He has served as UNESCO/UNDP advisor to the Ministry of Economic Development and Planning of Mauritius (1971-73) and as a delegate to the U.N. Conference on the Human Environment, Stockholm, 1972. He is at present working on two books, which are entitled* The Criteria of Development *and* The Political Economy of Food and Nutrition.

INTRODUCTION

LOUIS JUNKER

A new theoretical disposition seems to be slowly and, perhaps, reluctantly emerging and synthesizing in the analytical systems of the social sciences. It is a disposition whose terms are systems and networks rather than fixed elements and isolated compartments; motions and rhythms, ebbs and flows, rather than statics. Its subjects are relationships, transactions, and the analysis of power rather than final causes and fixed or neutralizing equilibrium; flows and feedbacks rather than essences; process rather than teleology. Its focus is valuational dynamics and commitments rather than neutrality and pseudo-objectivity in matters of values. It proceeds from concern with cultural evolution, institutional history and analysis, and the creative possibilities of warranted knowledge rather than from the simplistics of atomistic individualism and intellectual agnosticism.

Of course, these emphases are only some of our touch points, some of our cues to the emergence of a revolution in our thinking about the world and its problems. And, while it is true that no one scholar can encompass all aspects of this intellectual revolution in the making, it is imperative that we begin to sense its dimensions and importance, struggle with its emerging focuses and consequences, and eventually bring this new epistemological disposition to bear, not only on our limited worlds of scholarship, but on the everyday events of life, on the doings and sufferings of ordinary people in ordinary circumstances.

Against a large portion of this newer disposition stand the traditional analytical systems of the social sciences and especially the system of orthodox economic theory, which internalizes and retains most of the intellectual "tools" which the newer disposition regards as obsolete and even obstructionist. The consequences of this orthodox theoretical internalization and restriction are immense. Not only are orthodox practitioners of economics prone to confine their theoretical approach within narrow conceptual and disciplinary boundaries, they also would severely restrict our views of when a problem is or is not to be recognized as a problem. They show great reluctance to break out of the narrow parameters of the disciplines and recast old problems in a new framework, or to perceive and deal with newly emergent world problems from any perspective which might be more conducive than the orthodox perspective to identifying new problems efficiently and possibly to resolving them. This whole syndrome of theoretical defense and conceptual avoidance leads the discipline of economics and its orthodox devotees either to put real problems aside as non-problems, or to ignore them, misconceive them, or address them only within that obsolete theoretical system. The profession has shown a persistent habit, not only of making mountains out of molehills in its theoretical work, but also of making molehills out of mountainous problems in the simplistics of its policy judgements on matters of deep importance to humankind.

At this time and probably for some time to come, the world food and water problem, world hunger, problems of malnutrition and of protein and caloric maldistribution, and energy problems are increasingly severe; they demand center stage. These are mountainous problems. They are complex; we cannot even begin to address them without using some transdisciplinary methodologies. Yet, the professionals persist in conveying these issues to each other and to the public in mythological and misleading terms—in single cause–single effect methodological systems, with *ceteris parabis* assumptions and in static and comparatively static theoretical terms—when they attempt to relate their limited theories to such problems at all.

Our food system is all too often dogmatically hailed as the best, most nutritious, least denuded, contaminated and adulterated, best delivered, most worthy of being copied, most generous, and least wasteful food system in the world, without serious qualification. We are not required to assess the overall consequences of such factors as the massive unnecessary processing of our foodstuffs, our huge consumption of sugar, our lack of dietary fiber, the great use of food additives in our food manufacturing system, the ecological consequences of pesticides, herbicides, fungicides, rodenticides, etc., and the burgeoning growth of chemical food fabrication. We do not tend to carry out nutritional assessments and investigate pathological conditions on the basis of the effects of a consistent ingestion of a multiplicity of chemicals, nor do we deal effectively with the synergistic effects of those materials in the human body.

How often do we raise some important questions of the relationships between the small, rich portion of the world and the massive poor sections? How deeply do we examine the role of capitalistic enterprise and neo-colonialism, or the capacity of the rich to extract materials, resources, and even protein from the poor world? How often do we portray our agricultural system — the agribusiness complex — as the most efficient in the world without duly assessing the meaning of the word "efficiency" in the context of an energy criterion or evaluating its human consequences?

Our orthodox economic analysts have minimized the synergistic effects of a train of developments in the food supply system: the growing concentration of power in the food industries, the misuse of land, the destruction of the family farming system and the rising power of the agribusiness complex, and the role of corporate-directed media in shaping our lives, our diets, our attitudes and our perceptions of the world. Above all, these same orthodox economists have hewed to a thereotical approach which cannot deal with the gross and crucial problem of waste, or with the fact that our economic system has massive, programmed waste built into it at all levels.

How many economic studies have we seen on the problem of food waste in this society? How much do families waste? How much usable food from our restaurants, fast-food chains, and supermarkets ends up in the garbage cans of America? What portion of the hungry world could be fed with this wasted food? Only a few studies that I have seen try to assess the wastes caused by poor nutritional habits, which are often encouraged by the media. If we could adequately measure the unnecessary costs (waste) for hospital care, mental illness, allergies, diabetes, heart disease, artheriosclerosis, etc., due to the failure of the food system to supply the masses with life-giving foods instead of propaganda and misinformation, we would be doing useful economic analysis. To calculate the wasteful institutional patterns of a society is to calcuate social cost and the social burdens on its members. The problem of social waste and social costs treated effectively still presents itself as a new frontier to orthodox exonomics — never to be adequately handled so long as the dogma of marginal utility and free enterprise prevails in its present form. The outcome is the waste of human life.

Not all of these issues are dealt with by our participating authors in this volume, but one or another of them is analyzed from an unorthodox but most effective analytical position. Each one of the authors challenges some of the myths that prevail not only in our society in general but in the minds of professionals. Each one breaks new ground, ignores disciplinary boundaries, and uses transdisciplinary methodology to analyze the problems he addresses. In one way or another the work of these scholars, taken together as a piece, serves as a clear warning to all: Take action or perish.

It is bad enough that the odds are probably against us in this struggle to survive, for, as Thorstein Veblen observed when he wrote of how difficult it is to turn cultures around: . . .

> History records more frequent and more spectacular instances of the triumph of imbecile institutions over life and culture than of peoples who have by force of instictive insight saved themselves alive out of a desperately precarious institutional situation . . . [1]

At least let it be said that forewarned can be forearmed. With this introduction, let each of the authors speak for himself.

NOTE

1. Thorstein Veblen, *The Instinct of Workmanship and The State of The Industrial Arts* (New York: Viking Press, 1946).

WORLD FEEDING: FACTS AND FALLACIES

GEORG BORGSTROM

A number of facts are essential in understanding the world food issue. In too many instances the future outlook of this important aspect of our present world is distorted or presented in either too bright or too dim a light. We must find some middle road which is safely founded on fact, not fallacy; one that starts by accepting reality. I used to tell my students that facts are stubborn things and sooner or later they assert themselves. But much of the reasoning and projecting in the world food area has overlooked fundamental facts. Earlier editions of *Webster's Dictionary* defined insanity as the ability "to talk yourself out of reality." Much of what is written nowadays about the world food crisis raises serious doubts whether the author is of a sound mind. This brings me to a very basic point, with which I would like to start.

It is truly embarrassing to remind ourselves — embarrassing to the public debate and to the academic profession — that not more than ten years ago both professional journals and general news media were overflowing with articles about our glorious future. We were marching merrily together into a utopian paradise, characterized by limitless energy, unquenchable productivity, and, of all glories, almost limitless leisure. We were going to be paid negative income tax, a concept born in those days which means payment for not working, not producing, because we would be choking from an overflow of goods. You may have forgotten this, but I think anyone who starts reflecting remembers that this was the pitch.

That was the time when academia was garnished by study

1

groups about "post-scarcity" society. The movement started with a big national organization in 1964, and these study groups cropped up on a lot of campuses. These were the days when the secretary general of the United Nations, in one of his otherwise thoughtful speeches, happily told the world that we need not worry about the future, because we had reached the point in time and human history where resourcefulness would create resources. No one is denying the validity of this, but he did not point out something equally essential—that you cannot do a thing without resources. There is no use planning irrigation if there is no water within hundreds or thousands of miles, a situation now prevailing in many parts of the globe. When reading all those things I tend to think about the old battle hymn, "Glory, Glory Hallelujah." This was the march we were in, and it also applied to the food scene.

Not more than five years ago we were told and convinced that the green revolution had banished hunger from the poor world. And not only that, we were going to be favored with so much food through this development in the hungry world, so much grain, that we foresaw the spectre of burdensome surpluses, creating havoc for our own marketing of grain and other agricultural products. The poor countries were going to glut the cereal markets of the world, taking us back to pre-World War II, when the poor world was feeding the well-fed nations. It is embarrassing that we so completely lacked understanding of the basic parameters of our existence.

Then, in the beginning of the seventies, one crisis after another erupted on the world scene. The energy crisis, the food crisis, and the population crisis were dramatically brought to our attention. We started talking about how on earth we were going to handle these "problems." Two of them were highlighted in big meetings under the auspices of the United Nations: the World Food Conference in Rome, the Bucharest Conference on population, both in 1974, and the following year the Caracas Conference on the Sea, the biggest meeting the world ever held, with 7,000 participants. All three conferences were big rhetorical exercises. They pointed to important areas but made no real effort to find a viable pathway into the future. At the food conference there was one journalist for every delegate. Every golden word that the delegates said was saved somewhere in the records.

This is not the way to handle human affairs. You need no more than common sense and maybe a sliderule to see the true situation. We do not need professorial clubs, so-called Rome clubs, or others. Through the years many scientists have clearly brought out mankind's dilemma, but we have not paid attention to what they have said or written. I will give you one single reference. George Marsh, an American ambassador to Italy, wrote a book, *Man and Nature*, published in 1864, on the theme that we must economize with our natural resources, that we have to balance out the system so that forests do not vanish, groundwaters are not emptied, and topsoil eroded away. This book was reprinted in 1965 with the addition of seventeen footnotes—nothing more was needed to bring it up to date.

A colleague said to me recently: "It's amazing that the discussion about population and resources came that late."

"What do you mean by late?" was my question.

"Well, it really only started with Malthus."

He was obviously unaware that there was considerable concern about this matter already in the ancient world or of the lively debate on it during the 200 years prior to Malthus. On the third page of Malthus's *Essay on Population* (2d revised edition, 1803), the author refers to no less a personage than Benjamin Franklin, who came close to formulating the same law as Malthus did. Franklin simply stated that biological growth takes place in geometrical progression in contrast to technological growth, which proceeds on arithmetic progression. You have to add gallon to gallon of water, ton to ton of fertilizer, acre to acre of land, and so on. But when we made the energy input into technology we thought we had placed ourselves outside and above biological laws and our dependence on Nature.

I have prefaced my comments in this way because only five years ago we were made to believe that the duty of education was to prepare mankind for the shock of moving into a society called the After-Industrial Society, a society where there was said to be no scarcity. This was the theme of the bestseller *Future Shock* by A. Toffler (1972).

The Population Tide

What is the situation today? We face the unprecedented dilemma of adding more than a billion people in the next ten years. It took the world up to year 1820 to reach the first billion. (At the time of Christ world population was a quarter of a billion, a figure that did not double until about 1650.) Only in this very century did we reach the second billion (1930). The third billion emerged in 1960, by 1974 the fourth, and we will be adding 1,140 million in the next ten years. I doubt that any discipline has the slightest idea how we are going to manage this. We certainly are not taking action or formulating programs which can cope with this avalanche of people.

The world is adding the equivalent of a new United States in less than three years, a new Europe in six years. Asia is adding a new Japan each second year — each second year! The most rapid growth occurs in the southern portion of our own hemisphere, in Latin America, which is expected to add more than 300 million people before the year 2000. Brazil currently adds far more people to its population each year than does the Soviet Union, an empire of more than a quarter of a billion. Mexico is adding more people than is the United States. So is Nigeria. Africa will surpass Europe by 275 million before the end of this century.

As a visiting professor at the University of New Mexico a few years ago, I reminded my audience that the Mexico south of the border is growing per year by more people than the total population of New Mexico. That statement hit the public like a bolt, which to me proved that they had been unaware of this happening, verifiable in any statistical work and fundamental to them and their posterity. But the New Mexicans are not alone in their ignorance. Most of us are unaware of population developments equally ominous to our own future. We summarily talk about the population explosion, a highly inappropriate term. As the chemists tell you, an explosion is a one-time happening. It may be unpleasant when it goes on, but once it is over, you gradually pick up the marbles and start anew. But this is not what we are facing. We are facing a rising tide with no crest in sight.

Urbanization

This crucial predicament is compounded by the fact that in the next ten years around 750 million people will be added to the cities around the world, about 550 million of whom will be in the poor world. Some of this increase will be through natural growth, but the greater portion originates in an influx from the countryside. In the rich world a reduction in the number of rural inhabitants will partly compensate for the increase of city dwellers, but the poor world is playing the film backwards. The pressure on the countryside is forcing hundreds of millions into cities, requiring investments of a magnitude almost impossible to meet. In the meantime the rural population will continue to increase.

This ongoing urbanization is thoroughly restructuring the very fabric of today's society. It will compound the food issue and also add to food cost by exorbitant distribution burdens. The human misery and despair which follows in the wake of this process is beyond description. In Djakarta, Indonesia, a couple of years ago, I saw checkpoints established at the city borderline, manned by police and military personnel, to stop anybody from entering who could not show some documentary evidence of having a domicile or a job in the city. Most were turned away. Each day 600 came, a quarter of million in a year! In four years an army of a million of desperate, pleading people piles up in horrifying slums just outside the city. Someday these millions will undoubtedly march into Djakarta and take over the luxury palaces, the fancy insurance company buildings, and, in particular, the tourist hotels! This is a common situation in most of the poor world.

Despite the fact that chaos is imminent, the entire issue has been lift to Providence. Food, water, and, in large part, housing are taken for granted. Somehow we seem to believe that mystical market forces will automatically take care of these basic needs, despite clear evidence to the contrary.

Biological and Historical Dimensions

Why have we so completely failed to grasp the nature and the magnitude of this situation? I think that there are two fundamental reasons—lack of, first, the biological and, second, the historical dimensions in our image of the world.

Let us first look at the biological dimension, man's living domain, his biosphere, on which he depends for survival. The immediate part of that biosphere is livestock, which are fed in turn by plants, the feed crops. Man's living domain is therefore not limited to the 4 billion registered in population statistics. It is actually 5 times larger and should be considered to be 20 billion, because livestock, including poultry, account for 15 billion population equivalents (PE-units) on the basis of their protein intake. The United States today is carrying a feeding burden of 1.7 billion PE-units, including the 215 million people living here and 150 million in pets. In similar terms, India, representing three times more people, some 620 million, accounts for 1.4 billion, considerably fewer PE-units than the United States, a reflection of our substantially larger margin as to arable land, water, and other resources. If, as the rich world firmly seems to believe, it can uphold or even expand the present level of animal production, within the next ten years the world will be faced not only with filling the food needs of 1 billion more human beings but also with the requirements of the added livestock, the counterparts of no less than 4 billion PE-units. Thus the growth within the next ten years in biological terms is 5 billion, not 1 billion.

There are several indications we are not matching these gigantic orders and are failing to uphold this global standard. Despite expanding acreages in the developing world, its tilled land available per person is declining and averages only one-third of what is at the disposal of the developed world.

Now to the missing historical dimension. During the big European population explosion between 1850 and 1950, Westerners as a group grew more rapidly than any other branch of the human family. For two previous centuries Europe had persistently raised its food ceiling through agricultural advances, sucessfully battling limitations to the food supply. But around 1850 the population started to outgrow resources critically. Poverty, unemployment, and hunger embraced ever greater numbers, despite industrialization. The biggest migration ever in human history then took place. One-fourth of Europe's population migrated; 100 million left, 25 million returned. The poorhouses of Europe emptied onto the North American prairie. The flow of people also went to South America, the highlands of Africa, Oceania, and eastward to Siberia. As everyone knows, most of these regions had been colonized much earlier by European powers but were not truly settled by Westerners until 1850-1950. The North American immigration peaked in 1912. Scandinavian settlers had much more land on this continent than there was in the old countries totally. Sicily provided more people than any other island in the world, in relative terms, with Ireland a good runner-up. A major portion of the population in Brazil and Argentina are of German, Italian, and other European extraction.

In this grand, global operation Western man almost doubled his tilled land and more than trebled his pasturelands, chiefly in advantageous temperate latitudes. The feeding base of the West was thus vastly expanded, removing in an almost spectacular manner all limitations to the food supply of the white man.

There were two dramatic consequences of this happening. During this 100-year period transcontinental railroads and trans-oceanic shipping were developed, permitting long-distance hauling of food and feed on a major scale. Hunger was thereby removed from the Western scene for the first time in history, both in Europe and in the United States, where it had not been uncommon, as anybody knows who has read Rolvaag's *Giants in the Earth* about life among Norwegian settlers in North Dakota a hundred years ago. Furthermore for the first time in history it became truly feasible to feed cities of more than a million. But, most importantly, these conditions established a world trade pattern which has been dominated ever since by the flow of food, feed, and other commodities between the rich countries and into them from the poor world. I will discuss this pattern in more detail later, but first let us deal with a parallel of our worldwide land grab since World War II.

The Ocean Grab

Never have I in my wildest imagination believed that we would be allowed to duplicate this great feat. Speaking at a Food and Agriculture Organization conference in Norway in 1947, I pointed out that we were now at the threshold of a new era in which the oceans were going to be mobilized to feed the hungry nations. Here was the last continent and the last, best hope for the poor world. How deadly wrong I was. It is true that, not long after, a great crusade started for the untapped resources of the sea. Often, especially in the beginning of the 1960s, the proclaimed goal was to fill the protein needs of the undernourished, a very soundly conceived objective per se. "Freedom from Hunger" was the catch phrase for this campaign. But it did not work out as conceived. The big land grab operation was repeated in the oceans; today four-fifths of the harvests end up in the rich world regardless of what countries do the fishing. A persistently growing percentage of the catches has gone into fish meal and fish oil, the oil to the fat industries of the well-fed countries and the fish meal into supporting broilers and hogs in the United States as well as in Europe and Japan.

Spearheading this great rush for the living resources of the oceans have been the Soviet Union, Japan, and Europe, both East and West, with Poland and East Germany leading the East, and France and Spain the West. The big fourth power was the United States, emerging as the biggest buyer on the world market of fish and fish products at $1.5 billion per year. Our own fisheries have stagnated, but, since we are able to offer high prices, we have become a favorable market for fish fillets and shellfish. More than sixty countries, the majority of them hungry, are providing us with shrimp today. Fishing journals around the world are discussing how poor America is going to be supplied with fish. Only in tuna fisheries have we tried to keep up by modernizing and enlarging our fleet. Our average consumption is three pounds per person a year of "chicken of the sea," as tuna was labelled early by the commercial interests. Multiply that figure by 215 million and, in addition, by two since half the weight of the fish is bones, skin, viscera, etc., and you may understand why there is not enough tuna in the seas to sustain comparable consumption by another, equally populous nation − as the Soviet Union found out when it started a drive to copy our tuna harvest. We are not catching all the tuna we eat by a long shot; we also are the biggest buyers of this seafood on the world market. We use 50,000 tons of this excellent food merely for catfood.

Signs of overfishing abound, not the least in shrimping. The developed world is clearly up against the limitations of the ocean's living resources. The scope of fishing operations is being constantly widened to all oceans of the globe. The present fleet is quite capable of doubling its catches, which, as most experts agree, constitutes the likely limit of the ocean. Despite this, more catching vessels are added each year, and, as a consequence, each fishing effort produces less return.

But despite the extremely skewed distribution of ocean resources, aquatic protein fills the gap between starvation and subsistence for no less than 1.5 billion in the hungry world. The ongoing "Law of the Sea" conferences (Caracas, Geneva, etc.) presumably will find themselves recognizing the rights of all nations, including landlocked nations, to share in the ocean harvests.

Trade

Trade has been the chief way of removing limitations to the food supply in the latest 150 years. But most discussions have centered around trade with the food-short world and have given a wrong perspective. Even in grains only about one-third of the trade has been from abundant to needy countries. Most transfers of food and feed in world trade have been geared to secure nutritional affluence in Europe, Japan, and, since 1972, also in the U.S.S.R. Aid deliveries have shrunk, and grain purchases by major developing countries like China, India, Indonesia, and others have fallen below net imports of countries such as Japan, the United Kingdom, West Germany, Italy, and, again since 1972, the Soviet Union.

Japan and Europe, which together contain only about one-third as many people as China and India, import far more grain than these two giants together. Even when the scope is restricted to wheat they jointly receive more. We must eliminate the myth of the poor world as dependent and the rich world as self-sufficient. The truth is the reverse. This realization is a major task for education and is essential if we are to discuss the world food issues in realistic terms.

The false notion currently prevailing is that the poor countries by and large are net importers. The dominance of relief deliveries and concessionary sales has greatly contributed to this fallacy, resulting in the common assertion: "It is high time the poor countries learn how to get along on their own." The reverse statement would be more apropos. Outside of North America and Oceania, only France, Hungary, and Ireland are net exporters in the developed world. Denmark is on the borderline, but its net contribution to the world household is quite modest, as it is top-ranking in per capita import of feed protein. Most countries of the affluent world are in effect big net importers, accounting in each nation for large additional acreages on which they are depending.

China and India are right on balance. Their food imports are rather modest in relative terms and are counterbalanced — by exports of rice, eggs, and dried milk in the case of China, and by peanut cake and meal for India. Most of the African countries are net exporters. So is Central America, but under the pressure of growing numbers the choice there, increasingly, is between malnutrition and export earnings, which rarely benefit the victims of hunger.

The net-importing poor countries (in pounds per capita) are primarily those of the Caribbean, the Middle East, led by Egypt, and parts of South America. South Korea and Taiwan have swiftly lost their self-sufficiency (largely since 1965) and become increasingly dependent on long-distance hauling of food and feed. Japan, largely through heavy industrial overinvestment, has moved far into the red, and currently depends on a "ghost" acreage — i.e., agricultural land in other countries equal to more than three times its own tilled land. It has copied Britain and created world-wide systems of survival bases (in Canada, the United States, Ethiopia, Indonesia, Thailand, Brazil, Iran, Paraguay, and other parts of the world). In addition Japan depends on supplies from the oceans, a need which in terms of protein would require more than three times its presently tilled land to fulfill by way of its own agriculture. But in absolute figures Europe is the greatest parasite on the world household, receiving from overseas and from the oceans protein in an amount that would require more than half Europe's presently tilled land to produce within the continent. It thus depends on a sizeable shadow continent outside its own borders for its provision with food and feed.

The thrust of animal production is particularly evident in soybean trade. U.S. soybeans frequently have been touted as a major contribution to alleviating world hunger. This claim is highly deceptive, however, since only a fraction of the crop, even on the U.S. scene, is channeled into human food; most is fed to animals for meat production. The export by the United States of soybean protein as beans and meal with Europe and Japan as chief recipients carries the potential of supplementing the diet of no less than one and a half billion cereal eaters. But less than 5 percent of the exported soybeans currently serve this purpose.

To complete the picture it should be noted that 80 to 90 percent of animal products on the world market are sold to the affluent world. Only non-fat milk solids and some cheese have managed to break this trend. Much of the dried milk serves reconstitution dairies chiefly in Latin America and Southeast Asia which cater chiefly to well-to-do sectors within their respective countries.

The food luxury of the affluent world is primarily supported by the North American prairie. Of the grain deliveries in world trade, 88 percent come from the United States (75 percent) and Canada. We continue to talk about our grain deliveries as feeding the hungry world, but that accounts for only one-third of our grain exports. The other two-thirds, representing tremendous figures, goes to the well-fed countries, which, including ourselves, constitute only one-third of mankind, and the major portion of that grain is used as feed.

All these trade developments have protein as a key element. The large scale, long distance hauling of grain and oilseeds from the pampas and the prairies and of fish meal from the oceans is to obtain protein for animal production. The most serious side-effect of this extravagance has been that both Western man and the Japanese have lost all concepts of their own survival base as well as all touch with ecological realities.

The Gaps

What is the food gap? In terms of American standards, about

460 million people, or a little more than one-tenth of the world's four billion enjoy our average standard, that is, eat as well as we do. But please remember that people do not eat averages and there are lots of Americans who eat far below that level. Another telling measure is that if the total global food resources today were applied to give an American diet to as many as possible, only 970 million people — less than one-fourth of mankind — could be fed.

A comparison between the United States with 215 million and India with about thrice that number, or some 620 million people, provides another good illustration of the food gap. What we consume could, on the average Indian standard, feed 946 million, or about one-third more than India's present population. This is what we Americans represent in the world balance in food. And we are not alone in the Luxury Club. Europe's net importation of plant protein represents more than the whole African continent is eating as human food. Japan in a similar way buys from abroad about one-third the amount of plant protein Europe is getting, and this constitutes slightly more than the total consumption of plant protein as human food on the Indian subcontinent.

But there are other gaps. It takes 3,500 gallons of water to produce the daily food of the average American, including the feed crops. For a quart of milk one thousand gallons are needed; one single breakfast egg takes 120 gallons. If all this water were used to feed people at India's rate of consumption, it would be enough for one and half billion people. This illustrates the water gap, which in world-wide terms is much wider than the food gap between the developed and the developing nations. It also shows how extremely fortunate we are or how extremely wasteful we are, whichever way you want to put it.

The water crisis already looms large in many parts of the world and it will occupy the first-page headlines in our dailies within five years. In a great many countries, including our own, shortage of water is already, in one way or another, affecting food production adversely in increasing degrees. The U.S. Southwest is overusing its groundwater reserves, tapping annually what it takes one hundred years to accumulate. In parts of New Mexico the water table is already down to 1,000 feet, in parts of Arizona to 2,000 feet. Pumping from such depths is economically back-breaking.

Around the world big dams are being built on U.N. recommendations and often bankrolled by Western money or financed by the World Bank and similar international institutions, without cognizance of the basic prerequisite of whether the water will be there to fill them and without examination of the cost of distribution. This is why the green revolution is floundering. It is not based on genetics, the plant breeding science, so much as on the enormous inputs of water and fertilizers that it requires. Both water and fertilizer are energy-dependent. Even countries as affluent as our own can hardly afford this in the long run. Already even the richest California farmers pay only one-sixth of the true price of the water they are using, and we go out to tell the world they should copy this practice. We are now discussing how *we* are going to manage. Recently I was speaking about this to a big audience in Canada and the question was raised: When is the United States going to attack Canada in order to get water? This is a critical issue and already the sharpest diplomatic notes exchanged between Washington and Ottawa concern the water issue—Lake Michigan, the crossborder rivers in the Northwest, and the rivers flowing into Hudson Bay.

Justly may this century be labelled the Irrigation Century, having already increased the irrigated acreage world-wide four-fold and with a doubling of that projected before year 2000, when a total of 1 billion acres will be under irrigation. The International Hydrological Decade claims this is inadequate to meet the anticipated population growth.

Looking at other resources, such as forest products and metals, at our present level of consumption we Americans represent 10.5 billion Indians. But our energy consumption is the most atrocious. In this aspect of consumption we represent 15 billion Indians. Indeed, all these figures should in effect be increased, because the average Indian's life span is only two-thirds that of an American. The Europeans, who live generally as well as we do, use only half as much energy per person, which proves our wastefulness.

It is no wonder that the developing world has pointed out

these gaps at recent global conferences, and the same observations are now coming to the foreground in the General Assembly of the United Nations. For the first time we seem to recognize the validity of this criticism. And it is not only a question of criticism, it concerns the necessity of returning to a functioning world.

The 1972 crisis

What was the crisis of 1972 and how did we react to it? You all read about the droughts and floods that ravished large parts of the world that year. A broad belt around the globe was hit by severe droughts from Central America, across Sahelian Africa, India, China, and parts of the Philippines. Generally the droughts were followed by floods, which also destroyed much land. The U.N. Food and Agriculture Organization (FAO) reported that 44 countries did not know how to manage through the next year. Some 17 million tons of grain were urgently needed for relief purposes.

First of all, I wish to point out that we had precipitated this crisis. By "we" I mean the grain-exporting countries, above all the United States and Canada. Starting in 1969 and further in 1970 we reduced our acreages of wheat and other grains including corn, thereby reducing the world output by 25 million tons per year, much more than was needed to fill the immediate relief needs. This meant that our reserves were much below normal.

In the face of this disaster we instigated and were almost the sole decisive factor in what has been called the Soviet Grain Deal. It was a unilateral decision. I stress this, because it provides a good case to bring out the point that the world can no longer rely on unilateral decisions, whether they are made in Washington, Moscow, Peking, or some other capital. The decision was actually ultra-unilateral; not even the American Congress was consulted, much less the American people. And what did it amount to? The Soviet Union, hit by drought, bought 28 million tons of grain in the world market, the major portion, 18 million tons, from the United States. This deal was the biggest transfer of food and feed that ever took place in human history; it strained both land transportation and world shipping. In addition, the deal was subsidized by the American taxpayer at close to $400 million, since our wheat prices could not compete on the world market.

Was this good business? Yes and no. I want to stress emphatically that I have nothing against our selling of grain or other commodities to the Soviet Union. On the contrary, trade with the Soviet Union is absolutely essential and long overdue. But was it fair to a world in distress to empty our grainbins in this way in face of widespread disaster? The American grain reserve was what the world depended on for relief. Was it fair at this time to sideline our PL-480 program for food aid, devised in 1954, peaking in 1962, and gradually tapering off throughout the sixties? Furthermore, the Soviet grain deal caused a price spiral and thus the poor and hungry countries received even less grain than normal for the money budgeted for such purchases. The world crisis abated somewhat in 1973 because of better harvests, but a new severe drought hit in 1974. The Soviet grain purchases continued and have become a permanent feature in world trade. Nobody will ever know how many millions or tens of millions in the poor world succumbed as a result of our high-handedness.

The Soviet situation

The Soviet grain purchases in 1972 and later were not dictated by a need of staving off hunger for the nation. Our media tend to attribute them to Soviet agricultural incompetence. This position makes for good anti-Soviet propaganda, but we are fooling ourselves dangerously if we uncritically swallow such one-sided interpretations. There are several fundamental facts we should keep in mind in judging this situation. The Soviet Union is located almost entirely to the north of our latitudes, and half the land surface is under permafrost and cannot be cultivated. The U.S.S.R. also labors under much greater climatic adversities than do we. Yet we should not forget their impressive agricultural achievements during the postwar period, particularly the ongoing expansion into the vast parts of Siberia only recently taken into tilling. The Soviet Union is today the biggest milk producer in the world and is producing twice as much wheat as the United States. Throughout history right through the Stalin era, the Russians were restricted to a diet dominated by bread and potatoes. When Khrushchev came to power, he wanted to improve the dietary standard and successfully initiated a drive to increase animal production. The grain purchases in the world market are dictated by the desire to continue this ascent along the ladder of nutritional prodigality.

Our lavish banquet

The most critical aspect of the ongoing food crisis, however, is that the developed world has used its economic strength, as mirrored in mounting purchasing power and growing affluence, to strengthen its own food empire, and this has happened particularly since 1972. Never in my lifetime, in the thirty years I have been working in this area, have I seen a period so completely devoid of common sense and farsightedness as now.

To meet the growing markets, the United States removed all acreage restrictions, adding within two years 62 million acres to its tilled land, which corresponds to what France and England together have. Market forces were given practically free rein in adjusting production to demand, certainly not to needs of either the world at large or in the domestic arena. The result was that we in the rich world continued full speed to enhance our nutritional affluence with a consumption of animal protein already two to three times higher than needed. More and more grain, even wheat, is fed to animals. Feed crops are given preference over food crops.

In the midst of the most serious hunger crisis the world has ever seen, engulfing hundreds of millions of people, the rich and well-nourished nations, thinking only of themselves (pious declarations about development assistance to the contrary), have enhanced their own superabundance. This represents the most lavish banquet the world has ever seen and constitutes a challenge to all common sense, responsiblity, and progressive planning.

The United States, Canada, Europe, Japan, and the Soviet Union share the blame for these developments. They all acted in their own exclusive interests, oblivious to any obligations to the rest of the world. Two-thirds of mankind gets only one-fourth of the world's protein, mostly in the form of cereals. It is a case of the livestock of the affluent world versus the hungry millions. Yet, we are doing our very best to aggravate this confrontation in the 1970s by accelerating the expansion of our animal production while the countries of the poor world are forced to diminish theirs.

On top of this reckless behavior we engaged in an often offensive debate, repeating to a world in need that "it is high time you start taking care of yourself," which it is already by and large forced to do. New, arrogant concepts have been initiated such a *triage*, a French term, used in warfare by medical people who on the battle field must decide which victims may survive without help, which will die anyhow, and who may be saved only through immediate medical attention. We should then make the triage decision as to which hungry nations we should help to survive. Equally obnoxious is the lifeboat parable, or the decision of whom we should rescue by taking into our lifeboats. We, the rich countries, are emphatically not in lifeboats, we are steaming ahead in luxury cruisers supplied by delivery ships bringing in massive amounts of food and feed. We actually made our triage decision in the latter part of the sixties when a growing portion (up to 80 to 90 percent) of our steadily shrinking food aid was directed mainly to Indochina in accordance with our strategic interests. But the debate still continues along these lines. You hardly listen to a talk or read an article which does not have behind it the smug notion that there is a poor and backward world which is not capable of taking care of itself, while we are very much able to fend for ourselves.

The Rome conference

Finally, in the face of spreading starvation, the World Food Congress met in Rome in November 1974 to devise remedies. But, as I have already said, like all the other major conferences it removed itself to a comfortable distance from the acute crisis. Twenty-two very finely worded resolutions were made but not one concrete proposal. One potentially important decision was made, however. The World Food Council was formed under the United Nations with the task of creating regional emergency storages of primarily grain in strategic locations around the globe. The intention was that these stores should be kept filled by pledges from grain-exporting countries of certain deliveries on a continuing basis as needs emerged. But it has been more than uphill work, and so far only a couple of minor Western nations have made such pledges. The United States, the big grain empire and the largest exporter, had, at the time, emptied its grain bins and has so far not pledged a single ton. The whole effort is floundering, and the World Food Council is in limbo.

A New Strategy

The question is often raised, How many can the world, the United States, or some other given country feed? As everyone can deduce from my discussion, it depends on what dietary level we have in mind. Naturally the figure varies greatly, depending on whether we aim at the U.S., the Chinese, or some other food standard. In other words, it is a highly hypothetical question, leading to a rather futile debate. Instead of pursuing it, we should concentrate on the stern realities of today. Moreover we should not take refuge in talking about year 2000, or 2015, or some other arbitrary point of time in the distant future. We should tackle the task at hand here and now. We should start by recognizing the many fallacies prevalently accepted in a number of these areas today and by getting better acquainted with the true facts of our dilemma.

Our immediate task is to formulate a viable strategy for feeding and providing the other basics for those now living on earth or joining mankind in the next five to ten years. So far we have been good tacticians on many points, but an overall strategy has been woefully lacking in our endeavors. The food and population issue is not merely a matter of more food for more people or more food and strict population control to bring the two into balance. There are at least four other nerve centers to be coordinated in such a strategy, namely (1) reduction of waste and spoilage through improved storage and processing, (2) improved nutrition, (3) control of disease among man, livestock, and plants, and (4) better management of our natural resources in soils, water, energy, etc. We will discusss all six strategic elements briefly.

First, population control is indispensable and is well underway. The two-child family is already widely practiced in China, and there is a great likelihood that it will be proposed and put into law in India and Indonesia, as well. It is the rule in most European countries, and the United States is moving in that direction. But even if it is applied universally and immediately, the world will still be faced with a doubled population within 25 years. The braking distance is that long because the two-thirds of the world that is poor is a very young world, two-thirds are people below seventeen years of age.

Naturally we must make every reasonable effort to produce more food, but the biggest and fastest gains at the lowest cost would be achieved by cutting today's great losses in the world household caused by mismanagement, diseases, and pests. These are major threats right now; they should and can be reduced considerably. But I am referring especially to what is lost because of rodents, insects, molds, and other diseases and parasites which attack after harvest. These cause crop losses of between 30 and 50 percent globally (hard statistics on the matter are difficult to come by). The official loss figure for the United States as presented by our Department of Agriculture is about 30 percent. In the poor countries it may reach 50 to 80 percent. Great gains can be made in this area through proper storage, processing, and transportation facilities. Without producing one single ton more food, we could feed hundreds of millions more people by using such measures.

Even more appalling than such spoilage is the waste the rich world allows itself. Many European countries are feeding more skim milk to livestock than is consumed by their human population; some of it is even allowed to go out in the sewer, causing harmful water pollution. There are many countries in Europe feeding more fish protein (as fish meal) to livestock than fish protein to humans. This is part of the lavish banquet in which the rich countries indulge. We are all guilty of this and must retract, thereby releasing considerable quantities of food to those who need it.

To produce more food is not enough. It has to be the right kind of food, filling nutritional needs. While the average American is presently gorging himself on an average of 72 grams of animal protein per day, our nutritionists keep busy scaling down the theoretical minimum need from the presently established 20 grams per person a day—a highly devious, even cynical, way of "solving" the food crisis on paper and giving world dietary statistics an artificial face-lift. Instead we need some solid research into the consequences of overconsumption of such protein, there being many indications that it is directly harmful to our health. Under all circumstances a more equitable distribution is called for both within our country and globally.

Plans to produce more food must take into consideration the natural resources in soil, water, and energy, in other words, the ecological and climatological constraints we face. If we are going to bring food security to the world all these six elements must be coordinated. This is what economy is all about, and ecological balance is the basis for this coordination.

I would close by saying that we are at the end of a 500-year era, during which we Westerners have been living above our resources. That is the real reason for the inflation. Now we have to make needs and means meet. This is the basis of true economics, to balance out the system. In our economic analyses so far we have arbitrarily selected credit accounts in tonnage of food or ore, volume of forest products, amount of paper we have produced, etc. These figures have been climbing all along, and we have registered this as progress. But we left out the debit accounts in depleted and squandered resources in soils, groundwaters, forestland, minerals, and metals. This kind of dishonest bookkeeping must be stopped. In the rich world we have in later years revelled in what has justifiably been called a consumption explosion, paying little or no attention to the enormous unfilled needs of the two-and-a-half billion people on the other side of the gaps—the protein gap, the water gap, the energy gap. In all these key areas we have been doubling our consumption each twelfth year, thus widening the poverty gap. Some years our per capita *increase* has been higher than the total per capita consumption of the poor world.

A Marshall plan for the world is long overdue. It must include contingency storage of food, which has been calculated to cost around $5 billion a year, something we say we cannot afford. This brings up another point; our priorities are askew. The two superpowers and their satellites currently spend some $380 billion a year in the armaments race. This is more than the poor world is totally producing. After World War II, Senator Brien

McMahon made the wise proposal in the U.S. Congress that we should consider transferring one-tenth of the military budget into aid programs. This idea should be reactivated and made a part of the Marshall plan for the world. That is the only way to save our future and avoid a Third World War.

Finally, a general reflection: The most critical aspect of our cultural crisis is actually that we do not seem to care about the future. All civilizations including our own have been built on the very fundamental principle of improving conditions for posterity. All of a sudden we seem to have dropped this concern for future generations, discussing only how we are going to manage in our own lifetime or over the next ten years. Even worse, we seem to be fully prepared to do so at the expense of posterity, gobbling up and depleting resources at a rate unprecedented in history. If we do not change course, our entire civilization is doomed. But there is still hope and let us, by all means, get started in a better direction. We have no time to lose.

References

Lengthy reference lists and statistical material underpinning this article are available in my books:

Focal Points—A Global Food Strategy. New York: Macmillan, 1973, 320 pp.
World Food Resources. New York: Intext Educational Publishers, 1973, 237 pp.
The Food and People Dilemma. North Scituate, Mass.: Duxbury Press, 1973, 140 pp.

FARMING FOR PROFIT IN A HUNGRY WORLD:
THE MYTH OF AGRICULTURAL EFFICIENCY

MICHAEL PERELMAN

Agribusiness

American agriculture is big business. About 1 percent of all farms account for about 24 percent of all farm sales.[1] Many of these farmers are already quite well known. Dow Chemical, International Telephone and Telegraph Co., Coca-Cola (which owns Minute Maid), Gulf and Western, Kaiser Aluminum, Aetna Life Insurance, Goodyear, and Monsanto have spread their efforts into the countryside in search of profits. In California, 45 corporations now own 3.7 million acres, or nearly half of the farm land in the state.[2] On a national scale, two conglomerates, Purex and United Brands, now control about one-third of the green leafy vegetable production in the United States. Green Giant in Minnesota claims about 25 percent of the U.S. canned corn and peas market. Ralston-Purina, which had 1971 sales of some $1.75 billion and sells 14 percent of the U.S. livestock feed, is one of the nation's largest single producers of wheat, corn, and soy beans. Clifford Hardin, former Secretary of Agriculture, is now Vice-Chariman of Ralston-Purina, while the Secretary, Earl Butz, is a former company director.

Position of the independent farmer

Not only is an increasing share of farming directly controlled by major corporations, many of the apparently small, independent farmers are really not much more than corporate employees even though they might own hundreds of thousands of dollars' worth of capital. In the words of Earl Butz, the interest of the farmer will soon "lie in his rate of compensation per unit of product or per hour, as is now the case with much of our broiler production. In that case, the producer has about the same kind of compensation as does the worker in a Detroit automobile factory."[3] In fact, one of these broiler producers, injured at work, filed for workman's compensation arguing that he was no more than an employee of an agribusiness firm, and his claim was upheld by the courts.[4] Actually, the major difference between broiler producers and automobile workers lies in their rates of compensation. One Department of Agriculture study showed that the former managed to earn minus 36 cents per hour.[5]

Of course, not all farmers are impoverished. By 1973, the average income of farm families exceeded the national average.[6] But this income is not spread evenly. In 1972, the 5.9 percent of the U.S. population living on farms received only 3 percent of the national income for growing food.[7] Many, if not most, farmers have to supplement their income from nonfarm sources.[8]

The farmer finds himself squeezed on both sides, buying from and selling to monopolists, a hardly enviable position. For example, a 30-39 horsepower tractor in 1952 cost the equivalent of 1,283 bushels of wheat or 1,609 bushels of corn. Two decades later, the cost had more than doubled to 3,074 bushels of wheat or 3,291 bushels of corn,[9] while the monopolistic power of farm suppliers was further evidenced by the ability of the Soviets to produce tractors at about half the price of comparable U.S. equipment. [10]

Farmers, relatively devoid of any real power compared to their suppliers or the giant agribusiness middlemen, continued to fall behind in the competitive world. Only one avenue lay open— new technology. Modern labor-saving devices promised to cut costs and to improve their profit position. Work of every sort was mechanized. Naturally, the farm labor force fell.

Most of this farm mechanization was profitable only on parcels of land which were larger than average. The successful farmer was the one who could afford not only the new machines but also to purchase neighboring parcels of land to take full advantage of the new technology. As a result, the price of land was bid up. In fact, much of the profit on agriculture came in the form of real estate appreciation rather than as money profits. In 1973, for example, the increase in the value of farm real estate was actually 79 percent greater than the net income from farming.[11]

With the use of more and more expensive machinery and the soaring cost of land, the amount of capital tied up in a farm grew at breakneck speed. The amount of money which farmers needed to invest exceeded the amount they could save. They had to turn elsewhere for credit. As a result, farm debt has increased at about 9 percent per year since 1952.[12] Where banks were unwilling or unable to supply credit, farmers turned to suppliers or processors for credit. As early as 1964, the Department of Agriculture reported that crops grown under contract with processors or distributors had reached nearly 100 percent for sugar beets, castor beans, safflower, and hops.[13] Today we would add to this list broilers, fluid milk, vegetable seeds, hybrid seed corn, and vegetables for processing.[14] All in all, almost 20 percent of all farm output is grown under this sort of arrangement, which gives the creditor pervasive influence over farming operations.[15]

A few years ago you might have been shocked to hear about the manner in which corporate agribusiness firms abused their control of the market, but today our capacity for surprise is dulled; suffice it to say that the behavior of large agribusiness firms is typical of corporate behavior.

Position of the farm worker

As we mentioned before, the farmers generally tried to protect their position by mechanization; that is, in effect, by cutting back the share of agricultural income going to labor. As a result of this new technology, the share of labor in agriculture has fallen from 72 percent in 1949 to 33 percent in 1958.[16] The tomato harvester alone appears to have cost farm workers so much in lost wages ($43 million annually) that its net effect on society as a whole according to one University of California study may well have been negative.[17]

Since the purpose of mechanization is to rob Peter (that is, the farm worker) to pay Paul (the agribusiness firms), we need not be surprised that farm workers have not enjoyed the fruits of modern technology.

Males over 16 years of age with Spanish surnames earn only one-half as much in agriculture as in other industries.[18] Those farm-workers employed for a full year average little over $4,000 per year, while the average yearly wage for all farm workers taken together is about $1,100, according to 1972 figures.[19] Not only are the wages of rural workers below urban standards, but the cultural opportunities of rural workers are deficient.

Farmworkers' health suffers from continued exposure to pesticides, and the problem of pesticides is getting worse every year. Between 1966 and 1971 pesticide use increased by 40 percent.[20] The danger to farmworkers is disregarded, since the decision to spray rests in the hands of farmers whose million dollars' worth of pesticide applications are expected to bring in more than a billion dollars' worth of sales.[21] Empirical studies show, however, that a moderate cut back in pesticide use would result in more savings in terms of human health and environmental quality, measured by money costs such as medical bills, than the value of the production forgone.[22]

Reliance on Petrochemicals and Mechanization

With their machines fueled by fossil fuel and the chemicals they use manufactured from fossil fuel, farmers as a class have become a major user of petrochemicals. In fact, as Earl Butz has said, "American agriculture is the number one customer of the petroleum industry." No wonder! The dependence of U.S. agriculture on the petrochemical industry is so extreme that about five calories of fossil fuel energy are required for every calorie of food purchased at the store.[23] The chemical industry takes this dependence of U.S. agriculture for granted. In its view "the progressive farmer of today [is] an associated businessman in the chemical industry. After all, these men are producing proteins, fats, celluloses, carbohydrates—all of which are processed chemicals. . . . The goal of this chemical plant operator is not to grow a crop of lettuce, a herd of steers, etc., but to maximize his return on investment."[24]

For the sake of profit, agriculture has been transformed into an industry based on fossil fuel. The most prominent agricultural institutions have published mountains of information demonstrating the profitability of the new fossil fuel--based techniques; most large farmers accept this point of view, yet recent studies from Illinois suggest that organic farms are just as profitable as the typical commerical establishment. Since the organic farms get triple the value of product per unit of energy input (ignoring the higher prices of organic products), continued increases in energy prices should make them relatively more profitable in the future.[25]

That the organic farms can compare with farms using the widely accepted commercial practices is surprising because of the immense amount of research devoted to developing fossil fuel--based technology. Had comparable research been directed toward the utilization of manure, biological control, and the like, the results would have no doubt been more favorable to the organic methods.

This is neither the time nor the place to discuss an issue as controversial as organic versus chemical agriculture, nor should this be taken as an argument against a rational application of modern technology; the essential point to be made here is that the agricultural research establishment has been too close a working partner to the petrochemical industry. Agribusiness establishments have had influence in shaping the staffs of agricultural schools through grants awarded to those whose work merits their approval, and through hindering the advancement of those whose work is not deemed satisfactory with respect to their corporate interests.

The relationship between agribusiness and science is demonstrated amply by the ordering of priorities for research on alternative fertilizers. To illustrate this point, bear in mind that about 10 percent of all the money earned from the sales of a typical midwestern corn farm goes to pay its fertilizer bill.[26] Other nonmonetary costs of this technology exist, but their bill has not come due. Fertilizer salts percolate into the water table making drinking water potentially fatal for infants. Some evidence suggests that widespread use of nitrogen fertilizer threatens the ozone layer, which protects human life from dangerous ultraviolet rays. In fact according to one researcher, nitric oxide may by depleting the ozone layer three times faster than are aerosol sprays.[27] Furthermore, the energy cost of producing these fertilizers must be taken into account.

Given the $8 billion cost of nitrogen fertilizers as well as the problems resulting from their overuse, you might well expect a massive effort to harness the ability of certain strains of bacteria to "manufacture" fertilizer in the soil. Yet the Agricultural Research Service directed its research to what it called more pressing needs, employing only the equivalent of four full-time researchers in this area.[28] Incidentally, some of these more pressing needs include such work as arranging supermarket mirrors so that food appears more attractive and other worthwhile endeavors.[29]

Soybean farming

So that we can trace the logic of American agriculture, let us take a closer look at its handling of one specific alternative to chemical fertilizers, the soybean. This miraculous plant, so high in protein, is being counted as a potential solution to the world's protein problem. Yet soybean yields in this country have increased only slightly at about 1 percent per year.[30] Here again the Department of Agriculture employs only the equivalent of four full-time researchers on the improvement of all legume yields, not just the soybean.[31] Some observers hope that these yields can increase possibly through the introduction of new hybrid varieties. These hybrids, however, depend upon honey bees for pollination, and the honey bee is fast becoming an endangered species in America because of the intensive use of pesticides.[32] This problem cannot be taken lightly; fifteen percent of our crops rely on bees for pollination, and a total of about 33 percent of our crops depend on bees as a significant source of pollination.[33] Furthermore, a broad spectrum of creatures—from the microbial populations of the soil to our own persons—is affected by the use or misuse of pesticides.

Soybeans, however, are the second or third greatest user of pesticides of all crops in this country.[34] More importantly, soybeans have the ability to incorporate pesticides; that is, some insecticides sprayed on soybeans are found not only on the soybean but actually inside the soybean.[35] Finally, it should be mentioned that soybeans are very slow-growing crops. For this reason, land planted to soybeans has large amounts of bare and exposed area during the period before the maturation of the soybean, adding to the already horrendous problem of soil erosion in this country, where current data show that more than two-thirds of the crop land is in need of soil conservation.[36] (A few years ago the total mass of erosion from U.S. crop lands was estimated to be 4 billion tons;[37] increased mechanization and the use of herbicides rather than tilling has since probably increased that amount substantially.)

What has been said is not intended to downgrade the potential of the soybean. On the contrary, its potential is enormous. However, just planting more fields of soybeans is insufficient. A much broader perspective is needed. For example, the problem of soil erosion might be reduced if rows of corn were interplanted with the soybeans. Not only would the corn save the land, but an enormous amount of fossil fuel would be saved in the process. Further, the interplanting of soybeans and corn increases the total yield of the field; that is, while both the soybean and corn yield would be somewhat lower than the normal yield of either soybeans or corn, the total yield of both crops taken together would be substantially higher. Chinese farmers, for example, have recently amazed the American agricultural scientists, who calculated that their interplanting of corn and wheat gave approximately 40 percent more return than the traditional practice of planting a field to a single crop.[38]

The obvious objection to this system of cropping is that is makes mechanical harvesting more difficult. That is not to say that mechanical harvesting does not have serious drawbacks. Soybean farmers currently lose about 8 to 10 percent of their crop in the process of mechanical harvesting.[39] Large machines compact the soil, thereby inhibiting both root growth and drainage, and they exacerbate the problem of erosion. Furthermore, mechanization can create social problems, as we saw in the example of the tomato harvester.

On the other hand, this is not to say that all mechanical harvesting is bad or inefficient. Machines have the potential to free us from many burdens and tasks, although mechanization is not necessarily efficient. The case of the new lettuce harvesters, which depend upon x-rays to regulate the process of harvesting, comes to mind as a good example of a technology of doubtful social benefit.[40]

Technology and consideration of overall effects

What is required when the mechanization of soybean farming or any other technical approach to agriculture is discussed is a far-reaching analysis of the overall effects on all sectors of society as well as the environment. Take the introduction of the potato in Ireland as another example. The usual simple-minded discussion of the history of the potato in Ireland goes something like this: The Irish adopted the potato. The potato allowed them to feed the people. And finally, the potato famine came, causing the death of perhaps a couple million people. In reality, the introduction of the potato was a response to serious social disorders and its effects were also greatly modified by the existing structure of society.

The potato was adopted in Ireland because Ireland was a colonial power where soldiers marched and cavalry rode back and forth through the fields of the Irish farmers and commandeered grain wherever they could. The potato was an ideal defense. It was less easily damaged by trampling than wheat or other small grain crops. Further, potato crops need not be stored in warehouses, where they are easy prey for the enemy soldiers, but can be left in the ground.[41] So we need not be surprised that the potato was adopted in Ireland.

But what were the actual effects of the potato? The primary effect was to increase the number of people who could be fed from a single acre of land. Landlords were quick to capitalize on this property of potatoes. More rent could be collected if two families were to farm in the place of one. Increases in population were to the advantage of the landlords. And so we find in Ireland that the potential benefits from the potato were captured mostly by the landlord while the Irish peasantry fell deeper and deeper into poverty. All the while population grew. Then came the famine caused by a fungus to which the native plants from Latin America had been immune.[42]

A well-meaning technologist in Ireland could have pointed out at the time that the introduction of the potato would be an ideal means for increasing the people's standard of living; through the use of the potato more calories could be obtained with less work. But actually, such a recommendation would have been totally divorced from the social and political realities of Ireland. The question was not so much how to minimize the work required to produce food or how to maximize the output of food, but rather—at least the question should have been—how to eliminate the exploitation which kept the people in an artificial situation of poverty.

Even today in famine-struck Ethiopia, the most productive agricultural provinces suffer the most starvation. The reason can be found in the feudal structure of the society, where rents are commonly 75 percent of the total harvest.[43] Clearly, the political economy of agriculture can no more focus on purely technological phenomena than it can rely on simple-minded analysis of farmers' responses to the prevailing prices in the marketplace.

Implications of the Green Revolution

A modern example of the danger of purely technological analysis of agriculture is the so-called Green Revolution, which is the slogan given to the agricultural application of new Western-designed technology, which takes advantage of the intensive use of inputs such as fertilizer, insecticides, and machines. Ironically, the U.S. government official who coined the Green Revolution slogan was apparently ignorant of the fact that for about forty years his term had been used to describe a decentralized, organic form of life.[44]

From a technological viewpoint, nothing could be more reasonable; the United States is efficient in farming; U.S. farms are highly industrialized; therefore just transfer this technology to the Third World, where the U.S. experience can be duplicated. Unfortunately, life is not as simple as it appears to the technologists, and the problems of the Green Revolution are extremely serious.

To put the Green Revolution in perspective, we might consider what it would mean if the Indians were to adopt the same agriculture that we observe here in the United States. One economist, Folke Dovring, calculated that if the Indians were to have spent as much for fuel as U.S. agriculture, fuel costs alone would have totaled 4 to 5 percent of India's 1970 national product.[45] Now note these calculations were made before the recent skyrocketing in fuel prices. Furthermore, one recent survey indicates that mechanized Indian farms actually use more energy per acre than do U.S. farms.[46] If Indian farmers were to have spent as much as U.S. farmers on depreciation and repairs of farm machinery, these costs together with the costs of fuel would have totaled more than 10 percent of India's 1970 national product. Again, these calculations are based on data which predate the recent surge in inflation.[47]

However, India's population is two and one-half times as large as the U.S. population. In other words, in 1970 when the Green Revolution seemed to make a lot more sense economically, fuel and machinery costs alone would have required 25 percent of India's national product, assuming that the costs of Indian agriculture were equivalent to comparable U.S. costs per capita.

As implied earlier in my discussion on petroleum, the scarcity of resources world-wide precludes adoption of American agriculture throughout the world, just as the standard of living of this nation would be impossible for all nations to achieve simultaneously.

Many commentators gloss over this problem by arguing that U.S. agriculture directly consumes only a small fraction of the national energy budget, forgetting that when the indirect energy budget, including transportation, processing, and the like, is considered the food sector's share of the national energy budget swells to about 13 percent.[48] The monetary value of the energy spent in our food system totaled about $600 per capita in 1970, larger than the average gross domestic product of more than 30 nations.[49] What would happen if all nations tried to duplicate the U.S. food system? For example, if every nation in the world were to adopt U.S. agricultural techniques and if petroleum were the only source of nonsolar energy used, today's known usable petroleum reserves would be sufficient to farm for only 20 years, assuming no petroleum would be used for any nonfood related activities.[50]   Within this framework, the Green Revolution makes no sense at all, although for individual farmers, the Green Revolution may be very profitable indeed.

The efficiency of peasant agriculture

This conflict between individual profitability and the best interests of society as a whole rests at the heart of the problem. With the Green Revolution, modern technology threatens to force millions of small farmers off their land, making them into seasonal farm laborers or, worse yet, rendering them totally unemployed. Its promise to increase yields comes with an enormous price tag in terms of resource use.

To illustrate this price, consider the cost factor of inputs by farmers. In most nations this cost is equivalent to 3 percent of the national income. Yet in India these inputs purchased by farmers represented barely 1 percent of the 1963-64 net domestic product.[51] So simple calculations show how well India has economized on these purchased farm inputs. Since about 50 perpercent of India's net domestic product is agriculture, $1 worth of external inputs produces about $50 worth of food.[52] Whereas in most countries $1 worth of farm inputs results in only about $17 worth of food. David Pimentel and his colleagues at Cornell University calculate along these same lines that 1,000 kilocalories of plant food in India cost $10. The same amount of kilocalories in plant food costs $38 in the United States.[53] In part, these figures reflect a difference in dietary habits, but an even more important factor in the difference is the economy of Indian agriculture. Thus, Indian agriculture may be badly starved of external inputs, but the inputs that are made available to the Indian peasants are used quite efficiently.

Few Western economists have understood the efficiency of peasant agriculture and how few demands it makes on the industrialized sector of the economy.

The success of peasant agriculture can be judged, in part, by the amount of food the landlord can extract and the Ethiopian example above is not exceptional.[54] Furthermore, the achievements of the peasant must be judged in light of the fact that the best land was reserved for the wealthy growers, or in the case of tropical lands, for the multinational corporations which grow bananas, tea, rubber, and other exportable crops.[55] The peasants eke out their living on the most inferior soils, often on mountainsides. Given more land, along with a reduction of rents, peasant agriculture has an enormous potential for improvement.

All this might seem pure fantasy if we did not have an example of a nation able to harness the power of peasant agriculture and to use it as the basis for economic development. A few years ago few of you would have been able to anticipate the country to which I am referring, but today, I believe, most of you will know it is China. Chinese agriculture has been able to produce on very marginal lands sufficient food to feed one quarter of the world's population.[56] Of course, we here in this country would not have to live like the Chinese if we were to take full advantage of the biological potential of agriculture. To give you some idea of what the Chinese are achieving today, consider that the Chinese population is about five times as large as our own and that most of them live in an area about the size of California. The Chinese have nothing to compare with our own corn belt or the fertile valleys of California.[57]

Peasant agriculture requires very little in the way of fertilizer, machines, or fossil fuel. It is well adapted to an age of scarcity. I am not suggesting that we should all live like peasants nor that we all have to, but we do have much to learn from them.

For example, the Sacred Cow of India, long the butt of Western jokes, plays a remarkedly sophisticated role in India's agricultural ecology.[58] These poor scrawny animals are the peasant's tractor, truck, milk factory, tractor factory when they produce offspring, leather factory, manure factory, fuel factory, and the list could go on. Even the meat is used. During times of stress, while most of the underprivileged face famine or death, the cow is likely to die as well. The ban against eating meat does not extend to the Untouchable, who occupies the lowest rung on the Indian social ladder. Untouchabes eat meat. That is not to deny that the untouchable should have access to a better diet than the carcass of a dead cow, but it does provide a better diet for them than if the cow were to be processed into a MacDonald's hamburger for the middle class.

One study tried to quantify the amount of energy required

to maintain these cattle compared with the energetic value of their work and products. According to this study, the efficiency of Indian cattle is about eight and one-half times higher than that of range-fed cattle in the United States; for grain-fed cattle, the ratio would be even higher.[59]

Potential costs

The biological, ecological, and economic implications of the Green Revolution are extremely serious. It is true that the Green Revolution has increased the amount of wheat and rice produced in Asia.[60] But it is also true that the adoption of this technology requires heavy government subsidies in the form of cheap credit, favorable foreign exchange rates, and high government support prices.[61] We must go beyond the figures to discover the causes of these increases. Much of the increase comes from the use of irrigation on prime agricultural lands.[62] Extending irrigation is expensive and some observers even question whether it is possible to continue irrigating without depleting the ground water.[63] Also some of the increases in yield have been purchased at the expense of proper nutrition. To begin with, the new varieties appear to have a lower protein content than the grains they have replaced.[64] Secondly, farmers have shifted from planting legumes, which supply a great proportion of the protein consumed in Asia, to planting wheat and rice, further threatening the protein intake of the people.[65] Finally, in parts of Asia like Indonesia where the people rely heavily upon fish for their protein, insecticides threaten to kill the fish or make them unfit for human consumption.[66] And perhaps most importantly, for those dispossessed or unemployed because of the Green Revolution, the drop in their incomes undermines their ability to purchase an adequate diet.

Many scientists worry about the intensive use of insecticides associated with the Green Revolution. Foreign chemical manufacturers already have dumped toxic insecticides on the Indian market which are banned in the countries where they are made.[67] Other scientists fear that the Green Revolution may turn into what they call a Brown Revoultion, a replay of the Great Irish Potato Famine. Because of reliance on only a few plant strains of similar genetic make-up, a single disease could threaten to wipe out substantial portions of a nation's food supplies.[68] For example, in the Philippines, a hybrid rice called IR-8, one of the new varieties, was hit by a disease called tungro. Most farmers then switched to a new variety called IR-20, which was resistant to tungro but was hit by grassy stunt virus and brown leaf hopper insects. So many farmers switched to a new variety called 1561, which resists the virus and the bugs but is not fully resistant to tungro. Now the scientists have come up with IR-26, which is resistant to almost all Philippine diseases and insects but is vulnerable to damage from strong winds during flowering.[69]

More frighteningly, since insects and diseases can breed faster than plants, any single variety is sooner or later going to fall prey to them. We have two lines of defense against plant diseases and insects; first, we can diversify the genetic structure of our crops so that any particular disease could only threaten a small fraction of the total harvest; and second, we can maintain as broad a genetic base as possible in the long run, so that the plant breeders can draw upon particular resistances or other properties of the plants in order to breed new strains capable of facing any contingency. Some plant breeders hope to maintain the genetic potential of crops in seed banks, but obviously they could never preserve the genetic diversity incorporated in the 600 varieties of traditional rice strains grown in Indonesia or the 1200 grown in Bangladesh.[70] Besides the obvious problem that no one can predict which qualities should be selected for the seed banks, which have only a limited storage capacity, the seed banks themselves are dependent upon unforeseen occurances — such as the failure of three refrigerator compressors, which resulted in the loss of a major Peruvian collection of corn germ plasm, or the loss of some irreplacable corn collections during the reorganization of a seed bank in Mexico.[71] The Green Revolution threatens to reduce the wide genetic diversity of peasant agriculture to uniform strains of crops which are ideal for pest build-up.

Needed framework – social planning

Yet one nation has achieved many of the potential benefits from the Green Revolution with few of the associated costs.

The country is, of course, China. The reason why China has been able to achieve what has been mearly a dream for the rest of the Third World nations has been that she was not misled into any reliance on technology without a framework of overall social planning which made an efficient mobilization of national resources possible. In nations such as India, where each individual farmer is out to profit for himself, such overall coordination is impossible. Furthermore, the Third World countries launched their so-called Green Revolution under the shadow of the major capitalist nations of the world. In their state of poverty they had no opportunity to compete for the resources which were required to make the Green Revolution a real revolution. For example, the Green Revolution relies on extensive use of fertilizers. Yet the Indians do not have the money to purchase these fertilizers. In fact, the United States uses more fertilizer on its lawns, cemeteries, and golf courses than all of the farmers of the nation of India together have to use for farming.[72] The Green Revolution turns out to be a cruel hoax. Asian farmers who were induced to mechanize their harvests now have to spend four or five days waiting in line to fill a five-gallon can with diesel fuel while their American counterparts fill their giant machines to harvest tomatoes or grapes.[73]

The diverse paths which Asian and American agriculture were to take was seen very clearly by observers 100 years ago. Were we able to go back in time to 1873, we might hear C. L. Flint say to the Massachusetts State Board of Agriculture:

> If we are to support our present dense population, if we are to supply food with the present condition of our soil, we must go outside our own resources to do so. Up to this hour, farming in the United States has not been a proper culture but a system of soilation. Our population in the future must either starve or we must develop another course.[74]

That is, sooner or later, American agriculture had to begin to replace nutrients taken from the soil either by recycling them or by manufacturing them industrially. (While we do not have time here to go into detail about the costs of replacing the nutrients in the soil industrially rather than by way of recycling, we can mention in passing a few of the effects, which range from the poisoning of the ground water, eutrophication of rivers and lakes, and the upsetting of the ecological balance of the soil to the ultimate problem of the limitation of the resources required to produce these artificial fertilizers — due to most notably the limitations of fossil fuel and of the known reserves of phosphorus, which are expected to be depleted within the next 60 years.[75] Still parenthetically, we might also note that, while some people believe nuclear power can replace fossil fuel as a basic energy source, nobody yet has had the courage to to suggest that some substitute for phosphorus might be found.)

All these concerns are meaningless to the impoverished Indian farmer, who could in no way afford the costs of these expensive inputs. Again, going back in time to 1870 we might hear Lord Mayo stating "I do not know what is precisely meant by ammonic manure. If it means guano, superphosphate, or any other artificial product of that kind, we might as well ask the people of India to manure their soil with champagne."[76]

Now while it is true that India, for example, has been increasing its use of fertilizer over the last few years, it is also true that the further increase in fertilizer usage has been imperiled by decline in the stocks of Indian fertilizer, which have decreased by more than 1 million nutrient tons since the fiscal year of 1969-70.[77] Moreover, the use of fertilizer is not shared uniformly in India, nor has it ever been. As far back as 1928, the Royal Commission on Agriculture in India stressed the use of fertilizer "but applications until 1942 were largely limited to crops such as tea, sugar cane, and coffee," that is, crops which were grown by the large Western-owned plantations.[78] Of course, many Indian farmers with sufficient status or wealth will have access to more inputs, such as fertilizers, and many of them will find applications of such industrial inputs profitable, thus intensifying the gap between rich and poor. But once again we find that profitability has little to do with production. For example, the first pound of fertilizer applied to a farm will increase harvests more than will the thousandth pound or millionth pound applied. Therefore, if we are really serious about increasing the amount of food which the world can produce, we must find a way to distribute fertilizer stock as rationally as possible rather than having it applied intensively in areas such as Western Europe and the United States while large parts of the world receive no fertilizer whatsoever. In fact, Europe and North America together use about two-thirds of the world's total fertilizer.[79]

Before I continue our discussion of fertilizer, I would like to repeat once again that any serious response to the world food situation cannot be solely technological. It must take into consideration the social and political well-being of society as well.

Now, to get back to the subject of fertilizer, in my discussion of the importance of fertilizer to the Green Revolution I might have given the false impression that U.S. farmers have access to all the fertilizer they might want. Such is not the case. The United States has been short of fertilizer, and I suspect that further research will reveal the danger or even the presence of the fertilizer shortage to be as contrived as that of the so-called energy crisis. Over the past few years, American fertilizer producers have been shutting down plants here in the United States.[80] At the same time, commercial fertilizer corporations are building their plants abroad instead of in the United States.[81] For example, M. W. Kellogg & Co., the major builder of fertilizer plants in the world, presently has 40 new plants under construction or close to it. Only one of these is being built in the United States for an American fertilizer company and one other for a farm cooperative.[82] The United States is well on its way to becoming a major importer of ammonia-based fertilizers. One executive from Kellogg estimates that ten years from now we could easily be importing one-third to one-half of all our nitrogen fertilizers.[83] What assurance does the United States have that the major fertilizer companies could not orchestrate a new crisis, a major fertilizer crisis?

Once again we see the interplay between the purely technical aspects of food production and political realities. In this case these two influences meet in the proverbial conflict between guns and butter. For example, before the victory of the NLF, about one-half of all of our State Department--financed fertilizer shipments went to South Vietnam.[84] While this fertilizer may have been of some use to the Vietnamese, its main purpose was to serve the military and political goals of our government. Furthermore, the same chemicals which are used to produce fertilizers also are basic to the production of explosives. For example, 10-20 percent of the anhydrous nitrogen ammonia nitrate produced in this country is used for explosives,[85] and phosphates, too, are used for explosives. Thus, the choice must be made between the production of food which would feed starving people and the pursuit of still more military power. This dichotomy between guns and butter becomes apparent when we discover how some of the 355 U.S. Department of Agriculture specialists throughout the developing world[86] are used to support purely political aims rather than to improve the level of agricultural technology in the Third World. In a recent case, the CIA used the U.S. agricultural development organization to create a lucrative poultry farm for the Laotian general who ran the CIA-controlled army of Meo tribesmen.[87]

State of U. S. Food System

Not all the problems of agriculture are outside the borders of the United States. Even here, our ability to continue to produce food as cheaply as we have in the past is threatened. Valuable farm lands are converted into subdivisions and highways.[88] Other farm land is lost to erosion. Experiments with so-called modern technology, such as the supersonic transport, threaten to disrupt our agricultural potential. One study hypothesizes that the shift in atmospheric pollution caused by the supersonic transport alone could shift the northern boundary of the corn belt from Northern Minnesota and Southern Wisconsin and Michigan down to southern Iowa and central Illinois and Indiana as well as disrupting winter vegetable production in Florida, California, and the Southwest.[89]

Furthermore, many climatologists fear a deterioration in our weather. According to the estimates of some researchers, it appears that exceptional weather such as we have enjoyed over the last twenty years has played as important a role as technology in raising corn yields.[90] Since such good weather conditions historically last about twenty years, it may turn out that the climatic conditions to which our modern technology has been adapting are actually unusual, and so, with an unfortunate turn of the weather, we might have to fall back on our almost non-existent reserves of grain.

The true measure of efficiency in any economic system is the quality of the lives of the people affected by it. By this standard, how must we judge a system in which the average household puts about 15 percent of the dollar value of its annual food budget in the garbage can, including about \$100 worth of beef alone, while millions of people starve to death?[91] What does the milk used for nonfood sources here in the United States, two and one-half times more milk than all the people in the less developed world consume, indicate about the efficiency of the U.S. food system?[92]

This line of reasoning might seem inconsistent with the constantly repeated assertion that the U.S. food system is the most efficient in the world. But is it? Although it is true that U.S. agricultural yields have increased a great deal over the last century, much of this increase has been predicated on mining the soil and just plain good luck. One government report written at the turn of the century put the efficiency of U.S. agriculture in perspective: "The success and prosperity of the American farmer," it stated, "are due to the unbounded fertility of the soils, the cheapness of farm lands, and the privilege of using modern inventions and machinery rather than to systematic organization and efficient farm management."[93] Between 1900 and 1950, grain yields continued to increase by about 25 percent, but 40 percent of this increase came from reducing the planting on worn out soils and increasing the planting on more fertile soils.[94] Since 1950 it is estimated that favorable weather is responsible for about half of the further increases in yields.[95]

Finally, yield statistics are deceptive. A substantial portion of the increases in yields has been accomplished by shifting to lower quality plants.[96] As a result, the protein content of many modern grains is falling.[97] Between 1962 and 1973 the protein content of Montana wheat dropped by 6 percent.[98] Some wheat currently harvested in this country is so low in protein that it is unfit for milling, according to the U.S. Department of Agriculture.[99] Our fruits and vegetables are becoming more and more deficient in essential trace elements.[100] Even our milk is becoming less nutritious as Holsteins replace Guernseys and Jerseys.[101]

But the really revolutionary changes in American agriculture have not been directed toward increasing yields. As a comparison, Belgian wheat yields are double ours. Austria and Switzerland produce more corn per acre than the United States, and Egypt, Japan, Spain, and Australia produce higher yields of rice.[102]

Actually the unique achievement of U.S. agriculture is not the production of maximum crop yields but the harnessing of fossil fuel energy to replace human energy in agriculture. As we mentioned before, for each calorie of food energy produced in this country, a total of 5 to 10 calories of energy is required to run the farm machinery, to produce the insecticides, fertilizers and other farm inputs, and to transport the food and distribute it at markets.[103] In China, one calorie of human energy produces 50 calories of food.[104] In terms of energetic efficiency, it is 250 to 500 times more efficient than U.S. agriculture. Furthermore, U.S. agriculture's dependence on fossil fuels is increasing at more than 3 percent per year.[105] So in reality, the claim of efficiency turns out to be little more than reflection of a massive reliance on fossil fuel energy instead of on human labor power, the harnessing of potentially useful biological forces for control of insects or fixation of nitrogen. Furthermore, because the less developed nations have access to relatively little of the fossil fuel–based inputs, such as pesticides or fertilizer, shifting the use of these inputs from the United States abroad will increase the total amount of food produced.

Since little food is actually eaten on the farm, evaluation of our agricultural system must include the entire food industry. The 1967 Census of Manufactures showed 71 percent of the food industry profits went to only a hundred of the 32,500 manufacturing firms in that industry.[106] The Federal Trade Commission estimated in 1972 that the food industry had enough monoply power to overcharge consumers $2.6 billion for just 17 food lines.[107] About $2.3 billion is wasted for direct food advertising, not counting promotional gimmicks, excessive packaging, and stamps. While consumption of food in this country decreased in terms of weight from 1963 to 1971 by 2.3 percent per capita, packaging weight increased by 33.3 percent per capita.[108] For every dollar's worth of crops sold by farmers about 20 cents is spent for packaging materials.[109]

Another questionable area of the U.S. food industry is research. At present much of our research is directed toward increasing the profitablity of specific firms and industries rather than toward the interests of the nation as a whole. For example, intensive research was done to develop a tomato harvester just at the time when farm workers were beginning to organize in California.[110] The problems of the harvester mentioned earlier are compounded because the tomato must be bred to suit the needs of the machine, hard and impervious to bruising. As a result, they are artificially ripened by etholene gas, which reduces the vitamin A and vitamin C content.[111] Perhaps more importantly, they're tasteless.

Another example of the irrationality of agricultural research is offered by tomatoes. During the period 1960 to 1970, the number of tons of tomatoes purchased by California processors increased by 10 percent. The scientific efforts to improve tomato yields resulted in the addition of 450,000 extra tons to the 1971 California tomato crop—but this weight was all in the form of extra water. The individual farmer was rewarded for producing more water, but the processors who purchase about 86 percent of the harvest have to begin by removing this water so that the tomatoes can be converted to catsup, tomato sauce, and other products. Ultimately the consumer pays the water bill.[112] Perhaps the most important danger of this misorientation of our research effort comes in the form of deteriorating food quality.

In conclusion, our entire food system is in a shambles. Poor people are reduced to eating pet food while rich people can feed their pets in expensive restaurants. For the rest of us, the cost of our diet is increasing while its quality is falling. Food, a basic need of people, is being denied to millions and millions of people overseas as well as here in our own communities.

The efficiency of U.S. agriculture is a myth. Only when we cease to farm for profit in a hungry world and commence to produce for human need will an era of efficiency begin.

Notes

1. U.S., Department of Agriculture, Economic Research Service, *Our 31,000 Largest Farms*, by Radjoe Nicolitch, Agricultural Economic Report No. 175 (Washington, D.C.: Government Printing Office, Mar. 1970), p. 28.

2. Robert Felmeth, ed., *Power and Land in California*, p. 12.

3. Earl Butz, "The Appraisal of Land-Grant Colleges," *Banking*, Apr. 1962, p. 62.

4. Marcus vs. Eastern Agricultural Association, 32 N.J. 460, 161A, 2d, 247, 1960.

5. Harrison Welford, "Poultry Peonage," from his *Sowing the Wind: The Politics of Food Safety and Agribusiness*, reprinted in U.S., Congress, Senate, Select Committee on Small Business, *The Role of Giant Corporations in the American and World Economies*, Part 3: *Corporate Secrecy, Hearings* before the Subcommittee on Monopoly, 23 Nov. and 1 Dec. 1971, and 12 and 2 Mar. 1973, 92d Cong., 1st and 2d Sess., p. 3705.

6. U.S., Department of Agriculture, *Agricultural Statistics, 1974* (Washington, D.C.: Government Printing Office, 1974), p. 467.

7. *Ibid.*, pp. 433 and 467.

8. See R. J. Hanson and R. G. Spitze, "Increasing Incomes of Farm Families through Dual Employment," *Agricultural Finance Review* 35 (Oct. 1974): 59-64.

9. U.S., Congress, Senate, Committee on Labor and Public Welfare, *Farmworkers in Rural America, 1971-1972, Hearings* before the Subcommittee on Migratory Labor, 92d Congress, 1st Sess., held on 22 July, 21 and 22 Sept. and 5 Nov. 1971 and 11-13 Jan. and 19-20 July 1972, Part 4A, p. 2259 (hereafter referred to as *Farmworkers . . .*). Statement of James A. McHale.

10. Theodore Shabad, "Soviet-Made Tractors Introduced Upstate," *New York Times*, 24 Apr. 1973, p. 43.

11. *Agricultural Statistics*, 1974, pp. 427 and 467.

12. William McD. Herr, "Factors Affecting Annual Changes in Non--Real-Estate Farm Debt," Department of Agricultural Economics, Southern Illinois University, Carbondale, Ill., n.d.

13. William H. Scofield, "The Agribusiness Complex," presentation to the American Society of Farm Managers and Rural Appraisers, 1 Dec. 1969, reprinted in U.S., Congress, Senate, Select Committee on Small Business, *The Role of Giant Corporations in the American and World Economies*, Part 3B, *Corporate Secrecy: Agribusiness, Hearings* before the Subcommittee on Monopoly, 23 Nov. and 1 Dec. 1971 and 1 and 2 Mar. 1973, 92d Cong., 1st and 2d Sess., pp. 50, 68-71 (hereafter referred to as *Corporate Secrecy . . .*).

14. Leon Garoyan, "Is it Time for Contracts?" Presented at the Summer Institute, American Institute of Cooperation, Kansas State University, Manhattan, Ka., Aug. 1974.

15. *Ibid.*

16. T. P. Lianos and Q. Parls, "American Agriculture and the Prohpecy of Increasing Misery," *American Journal of Agricultural Economics* 54, No. 4, Part 1 (1972): 570-77.

17. Andrew Schmitz and David Seckler, "Merchanized Agriculture and Social Welfare: The Case of the Tomato Harvester," *American Journal of Agricultural Economics* 52 (Nov. 1970): 569-77.

18. U.S., Bureau of the Census, 1970 Census Population, Special Reports, *Industrial Characteristics*, PC(2) - 7B (Washington D.C.: Government Printing Office, June 1973), Table 44, p. 359.

19. U.S., Department of Agriculture, Economic Research Service, *The Hired Farm Working Force of 1972, A Statistical Report*, Agricultural Economic Report No. 239 (Washington, D.C.: Government Printing Office, Mar. 1973), pp. 5-6.

20. U.S., Department of Agriculture, Economic Research Service, *Farmers' Use of Pesticides in 1971*, Agricultural Economic Report No. 252 (Washington, D.C.: Government Printing Office, July 1974).

21. *Ibid.*

22. E.g., see Max R. Langham, Joseph C. Headley, and W. Frank Edwards, "Agricultural Pesticides: Productivity and Externalities," in *Environmental Quality Analysis: Theory and Method in the Social Science*, ed. by Allen V. Kneese and Blain T. Bower (Baltimore: Johns Hopkins Press, 1972).

23. Michael Perelman, "Farming with Petroleum," *Environment* 14, No. 8 (1972).

24. T. J. Army and M. E. Smith, "Research and Development in Farm Related Firms—Its Impact on Agriculture," *Structural Changes in Commercial Agriculture,* Report No. 24 (Ames, Ia.: Center for Agricultural and Economic Development, Iowa State University).

25. William Lockeretz *et al.*, "A Comparison of the Production, Economic Returns and Energy Intensiveness of Corn Belt Farms That Do and Do Not Use Inorganic Fertilizers and Pesticides" (St. Louis, Mo.: Center for the Biology of Natural Systems, Washington University, July 1975).

26. *Ibid.*

27. See Harold M. Schmeck, "Atmosphere Seen in Possible Peril," *New York Times,* 12 Dec. 1974, p. 50, col. 2.

28. U.S., Senate, Committee on Agriculture and Forestry, *Future Supply-Demand Situation for Fertilizer, Fuel, and Pesticides, Hearings* before the Subcommittee on Agricultural Credit and Rural Electrification, 93rd Cong., 2d Sess., 25 and 27 July 1974, letter of 9 April 1974, T. W. Edminister, Director, Agricultural Research Service, Department of Agriculture, to Senator George McGovern.

29. See Jim Hightower, *Hard Tomatoes, Hard Times* (Cambridge, Mass.: Schenkman, 1973).

30. *Agricultural Statistics, 1974*, p. 130. See also Lester Brown, "The Changing Face of Food Scarcity," Overseas Development Council, Communiqué No. 21, Aug. 1973.

31. *Agricultural Statistics, 1974*, p. 133.

32. Joseph M. Winski, "If You Don't Have Enough Woes, Try Fretting about Bees," *Wall Street Journal*, 7 Nov. 1974, p. 1.

33. University of California Food Task Force, *A Hungry World: The Challenge to Agriculture* (Berkley, Calif.: Division of Agricultural Sciences, University of California, 1974), p. 108.

34. *Ibid.*, p. 93.

35. U.S., President's Science Advisory Panel, *The World Food Problem*, Vol. II (Washington, D.C.: Government Printing Office, May 1967), p. 207.

36. U.S., Department of Agriculture, Conservation Needs Inventory Committee, *Basic Statistics of the National Inventory of Soil and Water Conservation Needs*, U.S.D.A. Statistical Bulletin No. 317 (Washington, D.C.: Government Printing Office, 1972).

37. U.S., Department of Agriculture, *Wastes in Relation to Agriculture and Forestry*, by Cecil H. Wadleigh, Miscellaneous Publication No. 1065 (Washington, D.C.: Government Printing Office, Mar. 1968), p. 6.

38. Royce Rensberger, "Chinese Farm Gains Impress Visitors," *New York Times*, 7 Oct. 1974, pp. 1 and 12.

39. "The Goal: Higher-Yielding Soybeans," *Agricultural Research* 22, No. 7 (1974).

40. "Harvesting Lettuce Electronically," *California Agriculture* 22, No. 7 (1974).

41. See Recliffe N. Salaman, *The Influence of the Potato on the Course of Irish History*, Tenth Finlay Memorial Lecture, delivered at the University College, Dublin, 27 Oct. 1943 (Dublin: Brown and Nolan, Ltd., 1944), p. 5.

42. E. C. Stakman, Richard Bradfield, and Paul C. Mangelsdorf, *Campaigns against Hunger* (Cambridge: MIT Press, 1967), p. 112.

43. Abraham Kidane, "The Political Economy of Famine: A Case Study of Ethiopia," presented at the 1974 Annual Meeting of African Studies Association, Chicago, 31 Oct. 1974, California State College, Domingues Hills, Processed, n.d.

44. The term was first used in 1940 at the suggestion of Peter Maurin at the School of Living, founded by Ralph Borsodi in 1940, to describe a decentralized system of agriculture. Later the term was adopted by The Catholic Worker. David Mitrany (*Marx against the Peasant* [Chapel Hill: University of North Carolina Press, 1951],

pp. 118-45), used the latter to describe radical peasant movements in Eastern Europe. William Gaud, Administrator of the Agency for International Development, first used the term to describe what the press now calls the "Green Revolution" in his address before the Society for International Development, "The Green Revolution: Accomplishments and Apprehensions," Washington, D.C., 1968.

45. Folke Dovring, "Macro Constraints on Agricultural Development in India," *Indian Journal of Agricultural Economics* 27, No. 1 (1972): 46-66.

46. Gajendra Singh, "Energy Inputs and Agricultural Production under Various Regimes of Mechanization in Northern India," unpublished dissertation, University of California, Davis, 1972.

47. Dovring, "Macro Constraints. . . ."

48. Carol Steinhart and John Steinhart, *Energy: Sources, Use and Role in Human Affairs* (North Scituate, Mass.: Duxbury Press, 1974), p. 340.

49. David Pimentel, *et al.*, "Food Production and the Energy Crisis," *Science* 182 (1973): 443-49.

50. *Ibid.*

51. Dovring, "Macro Constraints. . . ."

52. *Ibid.*

53. Pimentel, "Food Production. . . ."

54. Eric Axelrod, *The Political Economy of the Chinese Revolution* (Hong Kong: Union Research Institute, 1972), p. 49. For some additional comparative data see Cornell University Center for Environmental Quality Management, "Workshop on Research Methodologies for Studies of Energy, Food, Man and Environment: Phase 1," Cornell University, Ithaca, 18-20 June 1974. Also R. A. Berry, *Food Research Institute Studies* 12, No. 3 (1973): 199-232, and Peter Dorner, *Land Reform and Economic Development* (Baltimore: Penguin Books, 1972). For the effects of large Western plantation agriculture see George L. Beckford, *Persistant Poverty: Underdevelopment in Plantation Economies of the Third World* (New York: Oxford University Press, 1972).

55. See George L. Beckford, *Persistant Poverty: Underdevelopment in Plantation Economies of the Third World* (New York: Oxford University Press, 1972).

56. U.S., Department of Agriculture, Economic Research Service, *Agriculture in the United States and the People's Republic of China, 1967-71*, Foreign Agricultural Economic Report No. 94 (Washington, D.C.: Government Printing Office, Feb. 1974).

57. *Ibid.*

58. See Michael Perelman, "Sacred Cows," *American Journal of Agricultural Economics*, Aug. 1972, and "Sacred Cows: Reply," *American Journal of Agricultural Economics*, May 1973.

59. Stewart Odent'hal, "Energetics of Indian Cattle in their Environment," *Human Ecology* 1, No. 1 (1972): 3-22.

60. Lester Brown, *Seeds of Change* (New York: Praeger, 1970).

61. Walter Falcon, "The Green Revolution: Second Generation Problems," *American Journal of Agriculture Economics*, Dec. 1970. Also William Paddock, "How Green is the Green Revolution?" *BioScience* 20, No. 16 (15 Aug. 1970): 897-902.

62. Georg Borgstrom, *Focal Points, A Global Food Strategy*, (New York: Macmillan Co., 1973), pp. 177-81.

63. S. V. Ciriacy-Wantrup, "Natural Resources in Economic Growth: The Role of Institutions and Policies," *American Journal of Agricultural Economics* 51, No. 5 (1969).

64. U.S., Department of Agriculture, Foreign Economic Development Service, *Protein Supplementation: Satisfying Man's Food Needs*, by Aaron M. Altschul and Daniel Rosenfield, Bulletin No. 3, reprinted from *Progress* (the Unilever Quarterly) 54 (Mar. 1970): 76.

65. Alan Berg, *The Nutrition Factor: Its Role in National Development* (Washington D.C.: Brookings Institution, 1973), p. 58.

66. Richard W. Franke, "Miracle Seeds and Shattered Dreams," *Natural History* 83, No. 1 (1974).

67. M. R. Bhagavan, Kusha Haraksingh, Richard Payne, and David Smith, *The Death of the Green Revolution* (London: Haslemere Declaration Group, 1973).

68. H. Garrison and Susan Wilkes, "The Green Revolution," *Environment* 14 (Oct. 1972): 32-39.

69. "The Food Crisis: 'Green Revolution' Is Easing Hunger Slower Than Hoped," *Wall Street Journal*, 18 Nov. 1974, pp. 1 and 14.

70. Nicholas Wade, "Green Revolution (II): Problems of Adapting a Western Technology," *Science* 186 (27 Dec. 1974): 1186-92.

71. Garrison and Wilkes, "The Green Revolution," and Nicholas Wade, "Green Revolution (II)."

72. U.S., Department of Agriculture, Economic Research Service, *Fertilizer Situation*, 16 Jan. 1974, p. 4.

73. See Lewis Simons, "Fading of India's Green Revolution," *Washington Post*, 5 May 1974, p. C3.

74. See C. L. Flint in *21st Annual Report of the Massachusetts State Board of Agriculture*, (Statehouse, Boston, 1873), cited in National Academy of Science, Committee on Agriculture and the Environment, *Productive Agriculture and a Quality Environment* (Washington D.C.: By the Academy, 1974), p. 52.

75. The Insitute of Ecology, *Man in the Living Environment, Report of the Workshop on Global Ecological Problems,* 1971, pp. 48-59.

76. Cited in Stephen Merrett, "Indian Nitrogen Fertilizer Manufacture: Some Lessons for Industrial Planning," *Journal of Development Studies* 8 (July 1972): 395-410.

77. John B. Parker, "New Plants Up India's Fertilizer Output," *Foreign Agriculture* 12 (2 Dec. 1974): 4.

78. D. R. Gulati, "India's Food Requirement to Test Fertilizer Industry," *Foreign Agriculture,* 10 Dec. 1973, pp. 8-9.

79. University of California Food Task Force, *A Hungry World . . . ,* p. 97.

80. See "Fertilizer Capacity Can't Match Demand," *Business Week,* 17 Aug. 1974, pp. 25-26.

81. "Boom in Agrichemicals," *Business Week,* 8 June 1974, pp. 52-62, and "Fertilizer Shortage, How Bad Is It?" *Farm Index* 13 (May 1974): 16-18.

82. "Boom in Agrichemicals" (*Business Week*): 45.

83. *Ibid.*

84. U.S., Congress, House, Committee on Agriculture, *Fertilizer Shortage Situation, Hearings* before the Subcommittee on Department Operations, 93d Cong., 1st Sess., 26 Sept. and 3, 4, and 9 Oct. 1973, Government Printing Office, 1974, p. 12.

85. *Ibid,* p. 23.

86. Lyle Schertz, "World Food: Prices and the Poor," *Foreign Affairs* 52 (Apr. 1974): 535.

87. Arnold Abrams, "CIA's New Cover–Chicken Farms," *San Francisco Chronicle,* 3 Sept. 1974, p. 4.

88. See, for example, R. J. Arkley, "Soil Land Resources and Food," presented at the 1974 Annual Meeting of the American Association for the Advancement of Science, San Francisco, 28 Feb. 1974.

89. U.S., Congress, House, Committee on Foreign Affairs, *World Food Security: A Global Priority, Hearings* before the Subcommittee on International Relations, 93d Cong., 1st Sess., 31 July 1973, p. 80.

90. See L. M. Thompson *et al.,* "The Impact of Agricultural Drought in the Corn Belt and High Plains of the United States," A Report to the National Oceanic and Atmospheric Administration, 9 Nov. 1973, presently being rewritten for publication.

91. "How They Waste Food in Tuscon," *San Francisco Chronicle,* 14 Aug. 1974, p. 6, and William L. Rathje, "The Garbage Project," *Archaeology* 4 (Oct. 1974): 236-41.

92. U.S., Department of Agriculture, *Economics of Protein Improvement Programs in the Lower Income Countries*, by Lyle P. Schertz, Foreign Economic Development Report 11, July 1971.

93. Fred A. Shannon, *The Farmers' Last Frontier: Agriculture, 1869-1897* (New York: Farrar and Reinhart, 1945), p. 147, citing U.S., Dept. Agriculture, Bureau of Statistics, *The Cost of Producing Farm Products*, by Willet M. Hayes and Edward C. Parker, Bulletin No. 48 (Washington D.C.: Government Printing Office, 1906), p. 9.

94. D. Gale Johnson and Robert L. Gustafson, *Grain Yields and the American Food Supply* (Chicago: University of Chicago Press, 1962), p. 20.

95. See L. M. Thompson, Foreword to L. M. Thompson *et al.*, *Weather and our Food Supply*, Center for Agricultural and Economic Research Report 20 (Ames, Ia.: Iowa State University, 1964), p. i.

96. Michael Perelman, "The Political Economy of Food and Farming," unpublished ms., chap. 2, and "Farming with Petroleum," *Environment* 14 (Oct. 1972).

97. *Ibid.*

98. Charles F. McGuire, James R. Sims, and Paul L. Brown, *Fertilizing Montana Wheats to Improve Grain Yield and Baking Quality*, Montana Agricultural Experiment Station, Bulletin 674 (Bozeman, Mont., July 1974).

99. "More Nutritious Wheat," *Agricultural Research* 22, No. 9 (1974): 6-8.

100. Michael Blake, *Concentrated Incomplete Fertilizers* (London: Crosby Lockwood, 1967), pp. 14ff; and "60,000 EcoAcres," *Acres U.S.A.*, Dec. 1973, pp. 16-17.

101. See Pamela Hardt and Robert M. Shapiro, "Problems in the Dairy Industry," *Meta Information and Applications* (Wellfleet, Mass.) 20 May 1975.

102. *Agricultural Statistics, 1974*, pp. 5, 21-22, and 31.

103. See Michael Perelman, "Farming with Petroleum."

104. *Ibid.*

105. Quentin M. West, Administrator, U.S. Dept. of Agriculture, Economic Research Service, "Food Shortages: A Poor Man's Energy Crisis," presented at Oklahoma State Fair Energy Forum, Oklahoma City, 29 Sept. 1973.

106. Jim Hightower, "Feed, Farmers, Corporations, Earl Butz. . .and You," reprinted in U.S., Congress, House, Committee on the Judiciary, *Food Price Investigation, Hearings* before the Subcommittee on Monopolies and Commercial Law, 27 and 28 June and 11, 12, 16, 17 and 19 July 1963, 93d Cong., 1st Sess. p. 366.

107. Paul D. Scanlon, "FTC and Phase II: 'The McGovern Papers,'" *Antitrust Law and Economic Review* 5 (Spring 1972).

108. U.S., Environmental Protection Agency, *Second Report to Congress: Resource Recovery and Source Reduction, 1974* (Washington, D.C.: Government Printing Office, 1975), pp. 76–77.

109. Terry Crawford and Andrew Weiser, "The Bill for Marketing Farm Products," *Marketing and Transportation Situation* [U.S., Dept. of Agriculture, Economic Research Service], Aug. 1975.

110. Robert C. Fellmeth, *The Politics of Land: Ralph Nader's Study Group on Land Use in California* (New York: Grossman, 1973), pp. 60-64.

111. U.S., Congress, Senate, Committee on Labor and Public Welfare, *Farmworkers. . .,* 1972, p. 2291. Statement of Alice Shabecoff.

112. National Commission on Productivity, *Productivity in the Food Industry* (Washington, D.C.: By the Commission, 1972), p. 18.

THE STATUS OF COMPETITION IN THE FOOD MANUFACTURING AND FOOD RETAILING INDUSTRIES

RUSSELL C. PARKER

End of the era of low food prices

In 1975 Americans spent $209 billion on food and beverages. This amount was 21.7 percent of total consumption expenditures and greater than that for any other category of expenditure.[1] In the four years beginning with 1972, the amount consumers spent on food increased by 50 percent, principally because of higher food prices, and food prices became a major cause of inflation. In the single year between 1972 and 1973, higher food prices caused more than half the increase in the overall Consumer Price Index in the United States.

For a quarter of a century prior to 1972 a trend of slow-to-moderate food price increases caused a decline in the price of food products compared to other consumer products. This era of declining relative prices had seen the proportion of consumer expenditures for food drop from over a third at the end of World War II to less than a fifth at the end of 1971. Increasingly food became a bargain, according to a slogan widely promoted by the National Association of Food Chains.

Stable farm prices were responsible for the long, postwar trend of slower price increases in food products relative to other products. The U.S. Department of Agriculture index for the average farm price of raw food commodities in 1971 was identical to that of 1948. During the same period, however, the average price

51

consumers paid for food products in grocery stores increased 35 percent, and higher marketing margins, which rose over 80 percent during the period, were solely responsible. Had farm prices for raw foods increased at the same rate as the marketing margins, the average consumer price for food would have led the overall consumer price index (CPI) by a substantial amount rather than lagging behind as it in fact did.

Because of the slow growth in overall food prices, the growth in marketing margins was little noticed. As a result, food marketing was seldom in the spotlight of public attention, with the only noticeable exception coming when the short-lived National Commission on Food Marketing operated for a little more than a year during 1965 and 1966. Starting in 1972 food price increases changed this focus.

The very sharp increases in farm prices for raw food products which began in 1972 were passed on to consumers by processors and retailers. As they passed on the higher farm prices, processors and retailers also tacked on higher processing and retailing mark-ups. This pyramiding caused the annual rate of increase in food prices between 1972 and 1974 to exceed by five times the average annual increase over the previous twenty years. Between 1972 and 1974, the U.S. government's retail price index for food rose nearly three times faster than the index for other CPI items—a marked departure from the trend of the previous twenty years, when food prices had lagged behind the CPI by 25 percent.

The major factors leading to the higher farm prices in the early 1970s are now well known. They include world-wide feed grain and other commodity shortages; soaring petroleum prices, which increased not only energy costs but also the cost of hydrocarbon-based fertilizers; the devaluation of the U.S. dollar, which made U.S. food cheaper to foreigners; expanding real income outside the United States, causing further growth in foreign demand for U.S.--produced food; and the general inflation in the United States, which led to higher input prices for the food sector.

The reasons for the higher marketing margins charged by food processors and retailers during 1972-74, however, are less well known. The USDA index for food marketing margins[2] rose 31 percent during the 1972-74 period—a rate of increase nearly three times greater than the overall rate of inflation in the economy as measured by the rate of increase in the Consumer Price Index for items other than food. This paper reviews the trends in structure and performance in the food manufacturing and food retailing industries and examines the possibility of failures in competition as a cause of increasing marketing margins.

Food Manufacturing

The "Food and Kindred Products" major group of industries is the largest two-digit group within manufacturing. It employed 1.6 million persons in 1972, and its value of shipments of $115 billion was 15.2 percent of all manufacturing value of shipments.[3] Most of the forty-seven separate four-digit SIC industries that make up the group primarily produce consumer products—e.g., products such as breakfast cereals and canned fruits and vegetables that are distributed directly to consumers. The eleven primarily producer-goods industries among the forty-seven had a value of shipments which constituted only 14 percent of the group total shipments in 1972, producer goods being products such as cottonseed oil and soybean meal, which manufacturers sell primarily to other manufacturers for further processing. Most of the output of the consumer product industries is sold through food stores with the remainder going to restaurants and institutions. Food manufacturers supply about 90 percent of the food sold in grocery stores. The remainder is mainly fresh produce and fish and bakery products baked on the premises.

During the nineteenth century food processing and manufacturing grew rapidly to keep pace with the nation's expanding population, which was shifting away from farms and rural communities to large industrial centers. In recent years, increasing demand for prepared and convenience foods has helped sustain growth. As the food manufacturing industries became mechanized and as food manufacturers began to seek national markets, the food industries developed large-scale organizations. This trend became particularly noticeable in the 1920s and 1930s.[4] Since World War II the trend toward bigness and fewer firms has taken on a strong conglomerate character, which has caused major transformations in the structure of food manufacturing industries.

Number of companies declining

In contrast to all manufacturing, which has increased in number of companies, in food manufacturing, the number of companies declined between each quinquennial *Census of Manufactures* of the post–World War II period (see Table 1), and the rate of departure has been increasing.[5] The 1947 census enumerated over 40,000 companies in food manufacturing. In the 1972 census the number had dropped to 22,172. Between the two earliest post–World War II censuses the rate of decline averaged a little less than .9 percent per year. Over the most recent decade, 1962-72, the rate of exodus averaged 3.2 percent annually. If this trend continues throughout the next decade, half the current number of food manufacturers will disappear.

An analysis of the decline in company numbers between the 1967 and 1972 censuses reveals that the decrease was widely dispersed among the separate four-digit (SIC) food industries. Of the 42 four-digit food manufacturing industries defined within the two-digit Food and Kindred Products group for which a comparison could be made, between 1967 and 1972 company numbers fell in 33. Company numbers increased in only eight of the industries, and the increase for all eight was only sixty-eight companies. In one industry company numbers were constant.

Table 1

NUMBER OF FOOD AND KINDRED PRODUCTS MANUFACTURERS IN CENSUS YEARS 1947-72

Year	In Total of Four-digit Industries	Net of Duplication	Average Annual Change from Previous Census Col. 1	Col. 2
1947	41,147	N.A.	. . .	. . .
1954	38,610	N.A.	-.86	. . .
1958	36,545	N.A.	-1.31	. . .
1963	32,617	N.A.	-2.06	. . .
1967	27,706	26,749	-3.19	. . .
1972	23,326	22,172	-3.00	-3.21

Source: U.S., Bureau of Census, *General Summary, Census of Manufactures* for appropriate census years (Washington, D.C.: GPO), Table 2.

N.A.=not available

Plant size–declining cause of exodus

Although the disappearance of very small, inefficient-sized plants, particularly in the dairy industry and other local market industries, explained a large part of the early postwar exodus of companies, by the late 1960s inefficiency due to small plant size does not appear to be the prime cause of the increasing rate of company exodus. The twenty-four industries in which company numbers declined by over 10 percent between 1967 and 1972 were distributed randomly among all food industries with respect to average establishment size. The largest absolute declines in company numbers occurred, not unexpectedly, in the largest industries. Eight of the eleven industries in which company numbers declined by more than 100 during the period ranked among the ten largest food industries, and seven of the eleven showed either a higher percentage of larger plants disappearing than small plants or an insignificant difference in the rates of exodus by plant size.[6] Of further interest, in three of four industries having a significantly greater exodus of smaller plants than larger plants, the total number of companies declined more than the total number of plants, probably the result of acquisitions. Acquisitions would cause a decline in company numbers with smaller decline in number of plants if the acquired plants continued to be operated. In one of the three industries, soft drinks, the number of company exits exceeded the number of plant exits by seventy-three. This is an industry that experienced a substantial merger movement.

Both the plants and the companies in food and kindred products industries are larger than the average for the rest of manufacturing. The average value of shipments for food and kindred products manufacturing plants as reported in the 1972 census was $4.1 million, 85 percent larger than the plant average for all other manufacturing industries.[7] The average size food manufacturing company in 1972, measured in terms of value of shipments, was $5.2 million—twice the average size for companies in the rest of manufacturing.

Effects of high concentration of sales

The best single, generally available measure for evaluating competitiveness of industries is the level of market concentration. Market concentration refers to the extent to which only a few companies account for most sales or production in a market. The degree of product differentiation between the outputs of competing sellers (that is, the extent to which buyers prefer specific brands and the difficulty faced by outsiders who want to enter into a product area) is important, but this factor leads to, and therefore is highly correlated with, market concentration.

The level of concentration in a product market indicates the extent to which competing sellers are likely to be affected by the selling strategies of other competitors. For example, in the concentrated soft drink syrup industry, if Pepsi-Cola were undertaking a price promotion program to increase its share of the market, it would be vitally concerned with how Coca-Cola would counter in order to protect its market share. In unconcentrated markets each competitor is so small that possible competitor reactions are not a concern in choosing marketing strategies. A Kansas wheat farmer is not concerned about the production or marketing decisions of his neighbors, since the price he will receive is the result of interactions in a huge international wheat market to which he and his neighbors contribute only a minute amount of total supply. When concentration is substantial, however, the interdependence of leading firms is so great that competitors develop strong communities of interest in identifying and avoiding those actions most likely to produce competitive reactions which would result in reduced profits for all. Price rivalry is usually the first such action to be identified. This situation is called oligopoly. When concentration is great enough—that is, when firms can act without fear of effective dissent in achieving joint profit maximization—shared monopoly exists.

Sales concentration in food manufacturing

The Bureau of the Census computes concentration statistics which show the percentage of production or sales in a market accounted for by the four, eight, or twenty largest producers (four-, eight-, or twenty-firm concentration ratios). These measures are computed about three years after each regular Census year. The latest Census year for which complete concentration data are currently available is 1972.

Table 2 updates a similar table based on 1958 data appearing in the Federal Trade Commission staff report on the *Structure of Food Manufacturing*, published by the National Commission on Food Marketing as Technical Study No. 8. The table classifies food industries by level of concentration according to Professor Joe S. Bain's classification system.[8] Bain's highest concentration categories—very highly concentrated oligopolies (Type I) and highly concentrated oligopolies (Type II)—correspond to concentration levels associated with average profits which are significantly higher than those in industries with lower levels of concentration, according to the empirical relationship between concentration ratios and profit rates developed by Bain. A similar study of food manufacturing industries, reported in the FTC study on the *Structure of Food Manufacturing*, produced nearly identical findings. Thirty percent of all food industry value added and 25 percent of all food industry value of shipments fall within these top two concentration categories. Bain's two intermediate categories (Types III and IV) represent ranges of industry concentration in which profit rates increase significantly as levels of concentration increase. Three-fourths of all food manufacturing industries, three-fourths of total food manufacturing value added, and almost two-thirds of total food industry value of shipments fall either in these two categories of oligopoly or in the two highly concentrated categories. Only 23 percent of total food industry value added and 36 percent of total food industry value of shipments are from nonoligopolistic (i.e., competitive) industries.

Rising level of concentration

Between 1958, the Census data year on which the original table was based, and 1972, there were several definitional changes which make many of the comparisons between the industries in the Food and Kindred Products group either impossible or unreliable. However, a reliable analysis of concentration changes is possible for about half of the industries currently defined by

Table 2

FOOD AND KINDRED PRODUCTS INDUSTRIES CLASSIFIED BY BAIN'S CONCENTRATION TYPES, 1972

| | Number of Industries | | | Percentage of Food and Kindred Products Industry | | | | | |
| | | | | By Value Added | | | By Value of Shipments | | |
Bain's Type*	National	Local†	Total	National	Local†	Total	National	Local†	Total
I. Very highly concentrated	3	1	4	3	7	10	2	5	7
II. Highly concentrated oligopolies	8	2	10	11	9	20	9	9	18
III. High-moderate concentrated oligopolies	10	2	12	23	14	37	17	10	27
IV. "Low-grade" oligopolies	11	...	11	10	...	10	12	...	12
V. Unconcentrated industries	10	...	10	23	...	23	36	...	36
Total	42	5	47	70	30	100	76	24	100

Source: U.S., Bureau of the Census, *Concentration Ratios in Manufacturing 1972 Census of Manufactures* (Washington, D.C.: GPO, 1972), Table 5.

*Joe S. Bain, *Industrial Organization* (New York: John Wiley & Sons, 1959), pp. 124-33. Bain's type I, very highly concentrated class, includes industries whose top eight firms control 90 percent or more of production or whose top four control 75 percent or more. The equivalent percentages for type II are 85 to 90 percent for the top eight or 65 to 75 percent for the top four. Type III, 70-85 percent for the top eight or 50-65 percent for the top four. Type IV, 45-70 for the top eight or 35-50 for the top four. Unconcentrated industries would fall below type IV.

†Industries identified as local market industries in *The Structure of Food Manufacturing*, Technical Study Number 8 (Washington, D.C.: National Commission on Food Marketing, 1966), pp. 31 and 37. Concentration data for the five industries are from same source and *Economic Report on the Dairy Industry* (Washington, D.C.: Federal Trade Commission, 1973).

the Census. These are twenty-four national market industries whose definitions remained unchanged. Between 1958 and 1972, fifteen of the twenty-four comparable industries showed concentration increases of two percentage points or more, while seven industries showed declines of that magnitude. Five of the fifteen industries with concentration increases, however, registered increases of 14 percentage points or more, and none of the twenty-four comparable industries registered a concentration decline of that magnitude.

The change in weighted average concentration between 1958 and 1972 is shown in Table 3. The weighted average, four-firm concentration ratio for all national market industries, ignoring definition changes, increased from 39 percent in 1958 to 44 percent in 1972. Using estimates of average, four-firm, local market concentration for five industries, the weighted average, four-firm concentration ratio for all food industries increased from 47 percent in 1958 to 52 percent in 1972.

Underlying these average changes is much diversity. Willard Mueller has shown that the producer-good food industries have tended to decline in concentration whereas consumer products industries have increased.[9] The consumer products industries registering the largest increases in concentration were those with significant degrees of product differentiation as measured by the level of manufacturers' advertising expenditures—by confectionery products, coffee, beer, wine, and breakfast cereals, for example. Mergers also were important in several of these product areas. Significantly, industries in which advertising was less important experienced only moderate or no increases in concentration.

Some very important food industries—such as meatpacking, which fallis in the lowest differentiation category—experienced significant concentration decreases. Meatpacking companies account for about 10 percent of all food industry value added and nearly one out of every five food dollars spent by consumers. Since World War II, four-firm concentration in meatpacking has declined from 41 percent in 1947 to 22 percent in 1972.[10] The postwar decreases continued a trend initiated by the major antitrust actions in the industry in the early 1920s, when the industry was highly concentrated. Meatpacking is an industry in which advertising and other types of product differentiation activities

Table 3

WEIGHTED AVERAGE FOUR-FIRM CONCENTRATION
IN FOOD AND KINDRED PRODUCTS INDUSTRIES
1958, 1967, AND 1972

Year	National Market Industries*	National Market Industries Plus Average Local Market Concentration for 5 Industries[†]
1958	39	47
1967	41	50
1972	44	52

Source: U.S., Senate, Subcommittee on Antitrust and Monopoly, *Concentration Ratios in Manufacturing Industries* (Washington, D.C.: GPO, 1958), Table 2; and U.S., Bureau of the Census, *Concentration Ratios in Manufacturing 1972 Census of Manufactures* (Washington, D.C.: GPO, 1972), Table 5.

* Includes all food and kindred products four-digit SIC industries except Food Products not elsewhere classified and five local market industries. In 1967 and 1972, poultry dressing, egg processing, and frozen specialties were not included because of definition changes. The 1967 and 1972 data are for identical industries. 1958 tabulations use definitions which, in several instances, were changed by 1967. The purpose of the changes was to accomodate the changing character of products.

[†] Average local market concentration ratios for the late 1950s through the early 1970s, are as reported in the Federal Trade Commission staff report, *The Structure of Food Manufacturing* (National Commission on Food Marketing, 1966) and in the FTC staff *Economic Report on the Dairy Industry* (1973). The same average weighted local concentration ratios were used in both 1967 and 1972. The increase in the average between 1967 and 1972 was caused by higher national market concentration.

have declined and are currently unimportant. Consumers are aided in their purchase of meat by U.S. government inspection and grading. The story of the improving trend in meatpacking concentration has an interesting sidelight. In response to FTC actions that started the improving trend, the Commission and its staff were made the subject of McCarthy-type persecution by members of Congress who labeled the staff initiating the changes as Bolsheviks, demanded that they be fired, and caused the Commission's budget to be deeply slashed.

Multiplant operations

Notwithstanding the general increase in the size of food industry plants, scale economies at most explain only a fraction of the actual concentration levels observed in the food industries. In the twenty-three national market food industries with four-firm concentration greater than 40 percent in 1972, none of the top four firms operated an average of less than two plants. In sixteen of the twenty-three industries the four largest companies averaged more than four plants each, and in nine of the industries the four largest firms averaged seven or more plants each. The highest level of concentration justified on the basis of four plants of the average size operated by the top four firms was 43 percent. That industry was chewing gum, one of the very smallest food industries. The average level of four-plant concentration justified for all twenty-three concentrated industries was 15 percent, one-fourth the 60 percent, four-company level actually observed.

Because many of the plants operated by the four largest firms likely exceed the minimum optimal sizes for their industries, four-plant concentration of 15 percent is probably a substantial overstatement of the level of concentration justifiable strictly on the basis of plant scale economies. Diseconomies because of very large plants are not a problem in most food industries. Usually a food processing plant's production capacity can be increased without an increase in average unit costs simply by the addition of more production lines. Thus, as a company's sales expand in an area, it tends to accommodate the increase by expanding an existing plant beyond the minimum optimal size. On the other hand, it is very unlikely that the average size of plants operated by the four largest companies in food industries are ever reduced by averaging in the sizes of suboptimal plants since the four largest food industry companies should be operating few, if any, suboptimal-sized plants. If any of their plants were highter cost because of suboptimal-size, these multiplant firms would be free to close them and consolidate production in larger plants.

Large firms' increasing domination

Besides the high and rising level of industry concentration there also is a trend for a few very large companies to control production in all the food industries. The fifty largest food corporations owned 41 percent of all food manufacturing assets in 1950. By the end of 1974, this share had increased to 56 percent. The concentration of profits and of advertising expenditures is even greater than that of assets. In 1964, when the fifty largest companies controlled 49 percent of assets, they accounted for 61 percent of profits and nearly 90 percent of television advertising.[11] The trend toward increasing aggregate concentration is caused by increasing participation in multi-industry activity by large food manufacturing corporations. The individual industry positions held by large companies are leading positions. A special census tabulation for 1963 showed that only fifty food manufacturing corporations control 70 percent of the top four producing positions in all 40 individual four-digit food industries and nearly that percentage in the 116 five-digit food product classes.[12] Mergers since 1963 probably have further enhanced the very largest food manufacturing corporations' control of individual food industries and product classes.

Large company expansion through mergers

During the late 1950s and early 1960s, and coincident with an increasing merger trend for the whole economy, the merger activity of food companies accelerated rapidly. The increasing tempo of that activity in the years following 1963 (the year of the Census tabulation discussed above) and particularly the increasing acquisition rate of medium-sized and larger food companies began to threaten the survival of a viable middle tier of independent companies which compete with the very largest companies. As the trend of food company acquisitions continued its robust pace through the first half of the 1970s, aggregate concentration continued to increase, with the strong likelihood that leading positions in food product areas will soon be held by just a few very large companies. Many acquiring companies are not only large food manufacturers but also are huge conglomerate enterprises whose activities include nonfood grocery products and related trade and service areas.

The increase in aggregate concentration of food manufacturing company assets within the fifty largest food manufacturers between 1950 and 1965 was entirely the result of mergers. In fact, the 1966 FTC *Food Manufacturing* study shows that were it not for mergers the combined share of assets of the fifty largest food manufacturers would have declined between 1959 and 1965.[13] Although the data subsequent to 1965 have not been analyzed to indicate how mergers have contributed to increases in aggregate concentration in recent years, the brisk continuation of mergers, and especially large mergers, suggests that they continue to contribute to increasing food industry concentration. After 1965, the number of large food industry acquisitions increased not only absolutely but also as a percentage of all large manufacturing acquisitions (Table 4).

Prior to the mid-1950s many acquisitions had significant horizontal aspects. This trend changed as horizontal mergers were increasingly challenged by federal antitrust agencies. After the mid-1950s most food industry acquisitions were product extensions.[14] While these mergers added to aggregate concentration, they had no direct impact on concentration levels in individual industries.

The indirect effect of market extension mergers on industry concentration is another question. The 1966 FTC study on *The Structure of Food Manufacturing* reported that firms acquired by the fifty largest food manufacturers were typically large firms and were often one of the four leading producers in one or more food product areas.[15] Many were substantial advertisers of well-known food product brands. Within a year after acquisition, the acquiring companies doubled the average amount of advertising expenditure for the acquired brands, with television advertising

Table 4

LARGE FOOD MANUFACTURING COMPANIES ACQUIRED AS A
PERCENTAGE OF ALL LARGE MANUFACTURING COMPANIES
ACQUIRED, SELECTED PERIODS, 1948 THROUGH 1974

Period	Number of Years	Number of Large Food Manufacturers Acquired*	Percentage of All Large Manufacturing Acquisitions
1948-65	17	64	8.1
1966-68	3	47	12.1
1969-71	3	46	13.1
1972-74	3	29	14.4

Sources: National Commission on Food Marketing, *The Structure of Food Manufacturing* (Washington, D.C.: The Commission, 1966), Table 2, p. 110, and Table 4, p. 112; Federal Trade Commission, *Mergers and Acquisitions: 1972,* Table 13; 1973, Table 14; 1974, Table 14; also *Large Mergers in Manufacturing and Mining,* 1948-71, Table 3; and *Economic Report on Corporate Mergers,* 1969, Table 1-7 (Washington, D.C., FTC).

*Acquired firm's assets $10 million or more at time of acquisition.

showing the greatest percentage increase.[16] Although data on market-share change are not available, it is hard to believe that the additional advertising did not increase market shares and the level of industry concentration.

Another interesting fact reported in the 1966 study was that acquisition was almost the sole route by which the largest companies entered new industries. The FTC's detailed product data for the twenty largest food manufacturers showed that nearly 90 percent of the product areas entered by the companies were directly traceable to merger. Others that could not be definitely traced were most likely the result of merger. The largest food manufacturers' expenditures on research and development are consistent with this finding. In addition, Worley[17] found that, of twenty major industrial groups in manufacturing, only food manufacturing showed an inverse relationship between size of firm and the number of research and development personnel per 1,000 employees. The picture that emerges from these data and others, such as use of field sales force personnel and advertising, is that large food manufacturers move into new products only after they are developed by smaller firms. The acquiring corporations then enhance their newly acquired market positions through competition-reducing advertising and other forms of product differentiation.

Effects of lack of competition

To say that prices in an industry are too high means that costs and/or profits are in some sense too high.[18] Lack of competition can contribute to both higher costs and higher profits. Higher costs are produced by the lack of competitive pressures on managers to organize company operations efficiently and to oversee them diligently. Two hundred years ago Adam Smith noted this, observing that monopoly is "a great enemy to good management."[19] More recently observers have noted the tendency of oligopolistic industries to seek the tranquility of a "live and let live" existence and to avoid the threat of an outbreak of price rivalry by means of price leadership.[20] The implication of complacent conduct is not only higher costs in the present but even higher future costs because of the lack of progressiveness in the absence of pressure on companies to innovate. An important aspect of slow technological change is the continued high labor intensity in many food industries. The minimal research efforts of food manufacturing companies noted above does not suggest strong pressures for innovation; food retailers perform almost no R & D.

In the food industries, higher than competitive costs also result from high advertising and promotional expenses, packaging costs, other costs associated with creating product differentiation, and also from inefficiencies in delivery and service systems of some industries which are necessary to attract and hold certain classes of customers. The cost of maintaining excess capacity can be substantial. Excess capacity, particularly in the hands of larger companies, is a barrier to entry.

The main effect of the high promotion and product differentiation costs is that they cause consumers to have strong preferences for brands of particular sellers and most especially for brands of established sellers versus new entrants. This effect insulates the company that advertises against the encroachment of actual and potential competitors, giving it higher profits because of its ability to charge higher prices without losing market share.

Companies that are the heaviest users of advertising relative to sales are engaged primarily in the sale of soft drinks, confectionery products, and miscellaneous food products. In the 1960s, advertising as a percentage of sales for large corporations (over $50 million in sales) exceeded 8 percent in each of these areas.[21] It should also be noted, however, that several food industries have low advertising expenditures. These include companies producing producer goods such as sugar and flour, as well as consumer product companies selling fresh meats, white bread, or canned vegetables. For these products federal grade labeling or uniformity of product characteristics makes the creation of perceived differentiation difficult.

Advertising by food manufacturers increased dramatically after World War II. Between the end of World War II and the 1960s advertising doubled relative to sales for all food manufacturers. Although the rate has not increased as dramatically since the mid-1960s, the data picture is clouded by the increasing conglomeration of the largest food companies whose consolidated public reports give little or no information on their separate food industry activities.

Increasing profits

The profits of food manufacturers show a sustained upward trend over the last quarter of a century. Over the twenty-five-year period from 1951 through 1975 the profit rate of food manufacturers expressed as the ratio of after-tax profits to stockholders' equity increased by 50 percent (Table 5). The similar profit rate for all U.S. manufacturers over the same period showed no discernible trend. Average profits for food manufacturers were a fourth less than those for all manufacturers in the early 1950s. During the most recent five-year period, the average profit rate of food manufacturers exceeded that of all manufacturers by 6 percent.

Table 5

PROFITS AFTER TAXES AS A PERCENTAGE OF STOCKHOLDERS'
EQUITY FOR FOOD MANUFACTURING CORPORATIONS AND ALL
MANUFACTURING CORPORATIONS, BY FIVE-YEAR PERIODS,
1951-75

Five-year Period	Food Manufacturing	All Manufacturing	Food Profit Rate as a Percentage of All Manufacturing Profit Rate
1951-55	8.3	11.2	74
1956-60	8.9	10.3	86
1961-65	9.5	10.7	89
1966-70	10.9	11.6	94
1971-75*	12.3	11.8	106

Source: Federal Trade Commission, *Quarterly Financial Report for Manufacturing Mining and Trade Corporations* (Washington, D.C.: FTC).

*Includes only the first quarters of 1975.

Caution should be used in comparing reported profit levels of food companies with all manufacturers. Cooperatives, which generally do not have reported taxable income, make about 8 percent of the total sales of food companies.[22] Cooperatives make less than a quarter of 1 percent of sales of nonfood manufacturing companies. Another significant factor in determining the relative positions of food manufacturer versus all manufacturer profit levels has been the consistently low level of profits earned by companies in the very large, competitively structured, meat-packing sector of the food industries.[23]

Price fixing

Why are food manufacturers' profits higher than those of all manufacturers and increasing? A possible cause is explicit price fixing, which occurs when company executives meet secretly to set prices and market-sharing agreements. Not only does this kind of conspiracy still take place occasionally, but the records of antitrust actions show that some food industries have been prone to price fixing. Two food industries with such a history are bread baking and fluid milk processing. The high concentration in regional markets of these two industries and the relative similarity of products of rival sellers enhances the opportunity for such firms to collude and fix prices.

The *Bakers of Washington* case, successfully prosecuted by the Federal Trade Commission in the mid-1960s, is an example.[24] During the period of price fixing, the leading bakers of the State of Washington conspired among themselves and with the largest food chains in the area, one of which operated its own baking plant, and succeeded in raising the price of bread by 15 to 20 percent over a ten-year period extending from the mid-1950s to the mid-1960s. An antitrust investigation was ultimately begun, and upon conviction of the companies involved in the price fixing prices dropped. The Federal Trade Commission found that the wholesale bakers and the leading retailers in the conspiracy area had met frequently at state trade association meetings, and that, through agreements or understandings reached at those meetings, they had supressed price competition at both the wholesale and retail levels, and established and maintained uniform and noncompetitive prices. Figure 1 presents a picture of what happened. Prior to the conspiracy Seattle prices were nearly identical to the national average; during the period of the conspiracy prices were (as can be seen in the Figure) between 15 and 20 percent higher than the national average. Consumers in Washington paid approximately $30 million more for their bread than they would have if local prices had been the same as the national average during the period of the conspiracy. Following the conclusion of this antitrust action, vigorous price competition developed; the Seattle price immediately dropped well below the overall national average and, as time passed, it returned to the national average. It is interesting to note that, although vigorous price competition reduced bakers' profits, its main effect was to drive out inefficient firms and excess capacity that had been protected by the high price umbrella created by the conspiracy.

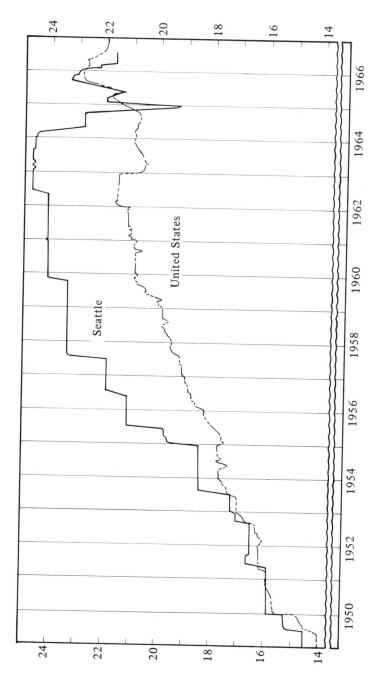

Fig. 1. Average retail prices for white bread in Seattle and the United States, 1950-67. (Source: Federal Trade Commission, *Economic Report on the Baking Industry* [Washington, D.C: FTC, 1966].)

The same Federal Trade Commission Economic Report that analyzed the Washington situation also reported the results of five other in-depth market investigations. These markets were chosen for study without regard to any information about conspiratorial conduct. In two of the five markets, analysis revealed prices above the national average or trends similar to that found in the *Bakers of Washington* case. In both instances, the Department of Justice brought suits and won antitrust victories. (In Baltimore, where price data subsequent to the suits have been analyzed, the average price of bread appears to have dropped approximately 15 percent, eliminating an estimated $5 million a year in consumer overcharge which had existed for a ten-year period.)

The frequency of explicit price fixing is not well documented since its clear illegality causes it to be cloaked in secrecy. Investigations are initiated only in the rare instances for which data show pricing patterns which strongly suggest collusive behavior or when someone priviledged to information about a price fix becomes an informer.

Oligopoly pricing

The preceding is an illustration of an explicit price conspiracy. Although I do not intend to minimize the importance of such conspiracies when they occur, structure-performance analyses indicate that tacit price collusion is much more pervasive. Tacit price collusion is typical in markets where there are few sellers, i.e., oligopolies. It results from the various forms of price leadership found in oligopolistic industries. A large and growing number of statistical studies demonstrate a relationship between the dimensions of market structure and profit rates, gross markups, and cost-price margins. The relationships are very similar in widely different industrial sectors and in statistical formulations that use different data sets and statistical techniques.[25]

The staff of the Federal Trade Commission conducted two analyses that are particularly relevant to the food industries. One develops the relationship between concentration, advertising intensity, market share, and the level of profits of food manufacturers;[26] the other employs a similar model in food retailing. The relationship for food manufacturing is summarized in Table 6.

Table 6

PROFIT RATES OF FOOD MANUFACTURING FIRMS ASSOCIATED WITH LEVELS OF INDUSTRY CONCENTRATION AND ADVERTISING-TO-SALES RATIOS

	Associated Net Firm Profit Rates as a Percent of Stockholders' Equity†				
Advertising-to-Sales Ratio (Percent)	1.0	2.0	3.0	4.0	5.0
Four-firm concentration:*					
40	6.3	7.4	8.5	9.6	10.7
45	8.0	9.1	10.2	11.3	12.4
50	9.3	10.4	11.5	12.6	13.7
55	10.3	11.4	12.5	13.6	14.7
60	11.0	12.1	13.2	14.3	15.4
65	11.4	12.5	13.6	14.7	15.8
70	11.5	12.6	13.7	14.8	15.9

Source: Federal Trade Commission, *Economic Report on the Influence of Market Structure on the Profit Performance of Food Manufacturing Companies* (Washington, D.C.: FTC, Sept. 1969), p. 7.

*The average concentration ratio (weighted by the company's value of shipments) of the product classes in which the company operated in 1950.

†Profit rates were calculated from the regression equation 1b shown in table 3-4, page 27 [in source]. Other variables influencing company profitability were held constant at their respective means. These variables were the firm's relative market share, growth in industry demand, firm diversification, and absolute firm size. Profit rates are averages for the years 1949-52.

When four-firm concentration averaged 40 percent and advertising sales ratios averaged 1 percent, companies earned an average profit rate of 6.3 percent. On the other hand, in industries where four-firm concentration averaged 70 percent and advertising expenditures averaged 5 percent of sales, there was an average net profit rate of 15.9 percent. Another variable in the analysis (not summarized in Table 6) shows that firms holding the dominant positions in the industries enjoyed even higher profit rates.[27] In short, these findings mean that the high frequency of moderate and high concentration industries in food manufacturing probably has a great effect on consumer prices. The Federal Trade Commission staff report was based on data from the early 1950s. Imel and Helmberger, using data from the 1960s, have observed a very similar relationship for that period.[28]

Grocery Retailing

Grocery retailing has experienced a major shift toward larger companies since World War II. This shift, which generally followed the "supermarket revolutions" of the 1930s and 1940s, saw concentration increase both in the nation as a whole and in individual city markets.

Large chains' share of sales

National concentration in grocery retailing is showing a strong upward trend. Just twenty large grocery chains accounted for 37 percent of total grocery store sales in the United States in 1975 (Table 7), an increase of more than a third over the 27 percent controlled by the twenty largest chains in 1948. The national concentration in grocery retailing increased despite the declining sales share of A & P, which until 1974 was the country's largest grocery retailer. Organized in 1859, A & P followed an aggressive course during most of the first 100 years of its existence. In the 1950s more than one out of every ten dollars spent in grocery stores was spent at an A & P (Table 7). Since then, and particularly since the mid-1960s, A & P's share of national grocery store sales has declined. Currently, its share of sales stands at less than 5 percent. A & P underwent a major reorganization beginning in

Table 7

MARKET SHARE OF TWENTY LEADING GROCERY CHAINS AND A & P, 1948-75

Rank	Percentage of Total Grocery Store Sales								
	1948	1954	1958	1963	1967	1972	1973	1974	1975
20 largest	27	30	34	34	34	36	NA	NA	37.0
A & P	11	11	11	9	8	7	6	5	4.9
2d to 20th largest	16	19	23	25	26	29	NA	NA	32.1

Sources: National Commission on Food Marketing, *Organization and Competition in Food Retailing* (June 1966), table 2-4 p. 41. Percentages for 1967 are based on Federal Trade Commission survey data for that year and Census of Business grocery store sales totals for 1967. The 1972 percentages are based on company data supplied to a Congressional Committee and data from the 1972 Census of Business, Retail Trade, *Establishment and Firm Size* and *Merchandise Line Sales.* Both the 1967 and 1972 percentages include sales of food departments operated in nonfood stores. The 1973 and 1974 percentages are based on A & P annual reports and grocery store sales totals reported in the Census of Business *Annual Survey* for these years. Percentages for 1975 were tabulated by the American Institute of Food Distribution and are for sales of grocery stores and food departments covering the period of Mar. 31, 1975, to Apr. 1, 1976.

late 1974. Post-reorganization operating results suggest that the company may be on the verge of halting its downward trend.

Sales concentration in city markets

Competition in grocery retailing does not occur at the national level except in procurement. Regional concentration is of importance because when grocery chains invade new city markets they usually do so from bases in nearby cities. Local concentration is of prime importance because the city or metropolitan area is the main arena of competition for consumer purchases. Few consumers consider traveling to another city to buy groceries. At the city level, concentration in grocery retailing is high and has been increasing gradually.

For the 200-plus standard metropolitan statistical areas for which the Bureau of the Census calculates grocery store sales concentration, the four largest grocery firms on average accounted for 52 percent of sales in 1972 (Table 8). In 1954 the four-firm average was only 45 percent. The eight-firm ratio increased faster—

Table 8

UNWEIGHTED AVERAGE GROCERY STORE CONCENTRATION
PERCENTAGES IN STANDARD METROPOLITAN
STATISTICAL AREAS, 1954-1972

Type of Concentration Ratio	1954	1958	1963	1967	1972
4-firm	45	49	50	51	52
8-firm	54	60	62	64	NA
20-firm	64	71	74	77	NA

Source: Special tabulations by the Bureau of the Census for the National Commission on Food Marketing and the Federal Trade Commission. Averages for comparable SMSAs.

from an average of 54 percent in 1954 to an average of 64 percent in 1967. (1972 data for other than four-firms are not available as of this writing.) The average twenty-firm ratio for grocery sales went from 64 percent in 1954 to 77 percent in 1972.

The Census tabulates sales of stores of voluntary and cooperative food chains on an individual store ownership basis rather than on a consolidated group basis. Although noncorporate food chains vary in the extent to which the actions of their individual member stores are coordinated, the Census tabulation method of always treating all grocery stores of noncorporate chains as separate units probably results in a significant understatement of the effective level metropolitan area concentration in a number of SMSAs.

On the average, Census concentration ratios are higher in smaller cities. To a significant degree this may reflect an understatement of concentration in large cities. Large cities, particularly very large cities such as Los Angeles and New York, are in fact comprised of distinct submarkets populated by different food chains and served by different advertising media. Concentration in smaller metropolitan areas also may be understated because of instances which include counties having a large part of their population in outlying areas.

The concept of all grocery store sales is too broad to define relevant markets. Most industry observers consider supermarkets as competing primarily among themselves. Convenience stores, such as 7-Eleven stores, and the large number of mom-and-pop stores that exist especially in central cities are considered in a separate category and not competitive in any substantial way with supermarkets. For example, the Supermarket Institute in attempting to measure the extent of competition faced by new supermarkets asks respondents to the SMI survey to list only the numbers of supermarkets. A special Census tabulation of grocery stores operated in four large, U.S. cities (New York, Los Angeles, Chicago, and Washington, D.C.) shows that supermarkets taking in over $1 million in annual sales made between 96 percent and 100 percent of the sales of the four largest chains in those cities. Whereas the four largest chains accounted for an average of 50 percent of all grocery store sales in the four cities, they accounted for 60 percent of sales of stores exceeding $1 million in annual sales. The same four chains on the average accounted for 70 percent of sales of stores with more than $4 million in annual sales. Because of the general bias toward underestimation of concentration levels, Census grocery store concentration ratios for metropolitan areas should be considered as minimum estimates of the actual level of concentration in metropolitan areas.

The national average of all cities hides the fact that in many individual metropolitan areas concentration is very high while in others it is low. Washington, D.C., has very high concentration (Table 9). In the Washington metropolitan area, four chains accounted for 76 percent of grocery store sales in 1972. The four chains accounted for 90 percent of the sales made in grocery stores with over $1 million in annual sales and for 96 percent of sales in those supermarkets with annual sales of over $4 million. Concentration in the Washington area food retailing industry is higher than that in nearly all manufacturing industries, including many that are considered virtual monopolies. Such high concentration gives the leading Washington area chains a strong position from which they could engage in tactics to discourage entry of new chains.[29] Denver, Colorado, is another highly concentrated, large SMSA. There the four largest chains accounted for 80 percent of total metropolitan area grocery store sales in 1972.

Major studies of grocery retailing, including those of the staff of the Federal Trade Commission[30] and the National Commission on Food Marketing,[31] have found significant barriers to entry created by, and significant pecuniary advantages of size inherent in the largest established food chains in local markets. Pecuniary advantages of large size are especially important in regard to newspaper advertising and procurement. The largest established chains in cities and regions also have advantages in the selection of store sites and, when their market shares are high, are able to use neighborhood pricing strategies that can discourage new entrants. Given these, there is little hope for a quick erosion of existing levels of grocery retailing concentration in metropolitan areas or even a dampening of the present upward trend.

Table 9

SHARE OF GROCERY STORES SALES BY FOUR LARGEST CHAINS
IN THE TWENTY LARGEST U.S. STANDARD METROPOLITAN
STATISTICAL AREAS, CENSUS YEARS 1954-72

Metropolitan Areas (Ranked by 1970 Population)	1954	1958	1963	1967	1972	Percentage Point Change, 1954-72
New York	41	37	34	33	31	-10
Los Angeles	30	25	30	28	36	6
Chicago	49	52	52	54	57	8
Philadelphia	53	60	61	60	54	1
Detroit	38	50	52	49	50	12
San Francisco-Oakland	27	29	33	40	41	14
Washington, D.C.	56	60	67	70	76	20
Boston	56	48	50	47	49	- 7
Pittsburgh	45	53	52	45	43	- 2
St. Louis	35	43	43	39	46	11
Baltimore	48	50	54	55	57	9
Cleveland	51	53	56	58	52	1
Houston	35	33	35	32	35	0
Newark	53	48	40	42	44	- 9
Minn.--St. Paul	31	38	39	44	42	11
Dallas	53	47	46	42	*	-11
Seattle-Everett	40	38	41	42	49	9
Anaheim--Santa Anna Garden Grove	40	47	43	39	44	4
Milwaukee	43	47	40	32	57	14
Atlanta	54	56	60	60	55	1
Simple Average	44	46	46	46	48	4

Source: Special Tabulation by the U.S. Bureau of the Census for the Federal Trade Commission. Data for 1972 preliminary.

*The Census merged the Dallas and Fort Worth SMSAs in collecting data for the 1972 *Census of Retail Trade*. The 4-firm concentration ratio for the combined SMSAs was 47 percent in 1972. The Dallas–Fort Worth concentration ratio was not used in computing the average for 1972 which was adjusted to be comparable to the 1967 average.

Markups

Approximately twenty cents of every dollar spent by consumers in supermarkets is retained to cover costs of operations and profits. The twenty cents is the average markup, which on food chain financial statements is referred to as the gross margin. On the average, a little over seventeen cents of the total twenty-cent gross margin covers operating costs and a little less than three cents generally goes to profits. The income tax rate on food chain profits averages slightly less than 50 percent, leaving a little less than one-and-a-half cents for after-tax profits. The total gross margin as well as the cost and profit components are each influenced by the competitive structures of grocery retailing markets.

The level of a food chain's gross margin in a city is strongly related to the share of the market it controls in the city. Tabulations of data submitted by food chains to the Federal Trade Commission (Table 10) and to the National Commission on Food Marketing (Table 11) show that grocery chains use higher markups

Table 10

DISTRIBUTION OF THE MARKET SHARE RATIOS FOR NATIONAL
TEA CO.'S OPERATION IN 399 CITIES, 1958

Market Share (in Percentage)	Number of Cities	Average Gross Profit Ratio	Average Contribution Ratio
Under 5	48	14.9	†(2.3)
5 to 9.9	93	16.4	1.0
10 to 14.9	83	17.0	3.7
15 to 19.9	55	17.0	4.0
20 to 24.9	47	17.5	5.7
25 to 34.9	44	17.5	5.5
35 and over	29	17.3	6.5
Total	399		

Source: Federal Trade Commission, *In the Matter of National Tea*, Docket No. 7457.

*Ratios in percentages. Simple average of the arithmetic means of the cities.

†Negative ratios in parentheses.

Table 11

ESTIMATED DOLLAR SUBSIDIES TO LOW MARKET-SHARE AREAS BY THE FIFTY LARGEST U.S. FOOD CHAINS

Market Share	Percentage of Stores	Gross Margin Index	Profits/ Sales Index*	Estimated Profit/ Sales Ratio†	Estimated Subsidy‡ in $ millions
4.9 percent & under	4	95	-78	-2.0	$ 92.0
5 to 9.9	13	98	41	1.1	97.5
10 to 14.9	19	99	64	1.6	95.0
15 to 19.9	24	100	100	2.6	...
20 to 24.9	9	100	116	3.0	...
25 to 34.9	17	100	119	3.1	...
35 and over	14	102	158	4.1	...
Total	100	100	100	2.6	284.5

Source: Russell C. Parker, "Competition in Food Retailing and Manufacturing," *The Market Functions and Costs for Foods between American Fields and Tables* (Washington, D.C.: U.S. Senate Committee on Agriculture and Forestry, 1975), p. 85.

*Average percentage of stores, gross margin index and profit/sales index for nine large food chains providing data to the National Commission of Food Marketing (index equals 100 for food chain average). Individual chain data are shown in Tables 10-5 through 10-13 (pp. 191 through 199) of Technical Study No. 7, National Commission on Food Marketing, 1966. In computing the nine-chain averages all chains were assumed to be of the same overall size. Market share averages were weighted by percentage of stores in market-share size classes. The average index for the nine chains was applied to average gross margin for corporate chains with over $100,000,000 in annual sales as reported in the Harvard-Cornell report, "Operating Results of Food Chains," 1963-64, Table 11-2, p. 222, and absolute margin difference was then applied to the estimated 1974 grocery store sales of the fifty largest food chains.

†Obtained by applying the average index for nine chains to the Harvard-Cornell series average before-tax profit/sales ratio for large food chains. Five-year average of data from Tables 13-6 and 13-11 of that series was 2.6 cents per dollar of sales.

‡Estimate based on the estimated 1974 grocery store sales of the fifty largest U.S. food chains. It assumes the nine chains are a representative sample of the fifty largest.

or gross margins in high market-share areas and lower markups where they have low market shares. This means that the price consumers pay for food retailing services goes up as the retailers' market shares increase. For the nine chains whose aggregated data are shown in Table 11, the difference in average gross margin between the lowest market-share class and the highest is 7 to 8 percent.

Gross margins

Average gross margins of food chains have been subject to significant upward and downward trends over the last several decades (Figure 2). Between the early 1930s and the early 1950s, the average gross margins of large food chains decreased from 23 percent to about 15 percent of sales. This large decline was caused mainly by the efficiencies introduced by the supermarket revolution. The downward trend ended in the early 1950s and reversed itself. From then until the late 1960s food chain gross margins increased, and by the late 1960s they had climbed back to the levels in effect before the supermarket revolution of the early 1930s. Beginning in the late 1960s gross margins leveled off and have since declined by about a percentage point.

The increase in the 1950s and 1960s was caused by many factors. Chains added in-store services and began to focus expenditures on other, nonprice elements of competition.[32] Among these elements were: (1) increased promotional expenditures on trading stamps and games of chance and (2) increased advertising expenditures. The introduction of trading stamps in grocery stores in the 1950s and 1960s cost chains not only the purchase price of the stamps but also the added expense of dispersing them at check-out stands. The total cost of stamps was frequently about three cents per dollar sales. As other chains adopted stamps, the sales volume increases initially realized by the originating chains disappeared and the total cost of dispensing the stamps had to be passed on to customers.[33] In addition, chains also began building more expensive stores and parking lots.[34] In recent years, chains have created considerable excess store capacity, referred to in the trade literature as overstoring. Overstoring caused cost increases much as stamps had. The report of the

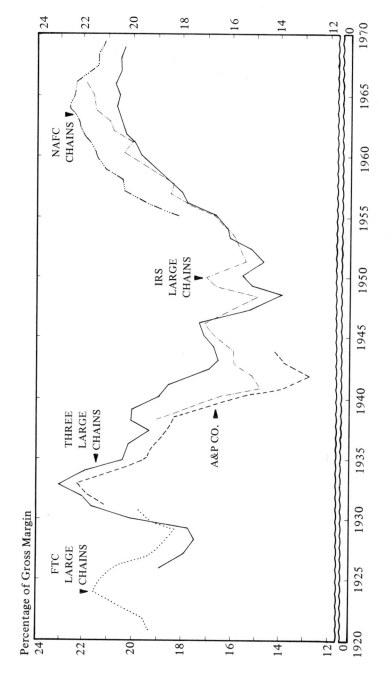

Percentage of Gross Margin

Fig. 2. Retail gross margins of large food chains, 1921-69. (Source: Staff Report to the Federal Trade Commission, *Discount Food Pricing in Washington, D.C.* [Washington, D.C.: FTC, 1971], Fig. 1, p. 17).

Canadian *Royal Commission on Consumer Problems and Inflation* estimates that excess capacity or "overstoring" in food retailing in Canada cost Canadian consumers "an average of four cents more than necessary per dollar of sales. ..."[35]

Underlying this shift from price to nonprice forms of rivalry, which resulted in higher costs and higher retail food prices, was an extensive merger movement in food retailing, which began in the 1950s. The increase in mergers and the increase in gross margins began almost simultaneously, the effect being to eliminate the procompetitive force of actual and potential entry of chains from nearby cities. This kind of entry is a very significant force in directing food retailers to compete on a price basis as a means of carving out and holding onto market shares. When large chains chose the merger route for expansion into new markets, price rivalry subsided.[36] In the mid-1960s, court victories in federal antitrust cases curtailed mergers. The leveling off and slight decline in gross margins in the final years of the 1960s and the early 1970s may be evidence that some of the price competition which had been muted by the merger movement had resumed.[37] Several of the most active acquiring food chains of the 1950s and 1960s continued their growth objectives after the new merger enforcement policy was achieved. In place of acquiring growing concerns these chains were forced to enter new markets by building new stores. To attract customers to these new stores, many of the new entrants offered themselves as low margin "discount" sellers. Since 1965, gross margins have not only stopped going up but dropped by a little more than a percentage point (Figure 2). Considering that annual grocery store sales are currently about $125 billion, savings to consumers because of the decline in margins since the late 1960s have probably been about $1.5 billion a year. If it is assumed that after 1965 food chain gross margins would have continued increasing at the same rate they exhibited during the 1950s and early 1960s, then the estimated annual savings to consumers as a result of the decline in margin is considerably more than $1.5 billion.

Retailing profit rates

Ratios of long-run profit to stockholders' equity have averaged

50 percent higher for food retailers than for other retailers. For the two decades from 1952 through 1971, the most recent year for which Internal Revenue Service data from corporate tax returns are available, food retailers earned an 8.9 percent average after-tax profit rate on stockholders' equity compared with 6.0 percent earned by other retailers.[38] Food retailers' rate of return averaged about 20 percent higher than that of food manufacturers over the twenty-year period.

Profits of large food chains generally averaged higher than other food retailers'. For the first part of the period, 1952 to 1964, food chains having more than $50 million in assets earned an average return on equity of 10.3 percent—15 percent higher than for all food retailers. During the seven years between 1964 and 1971, the average profit rate of large chains dropped to a level comparable to that of the industry as a whole,[39] the decline caused in significant part by the sagging profits of A & P.[40] Since 1972, food chain profits have been greatly affected by A & P's WEO discount program and A & P's massive accounting write-off in 1974.[41] Except for A & P, profit rates in 1974 and 1975 have shown a tendency to return to previous higher levels.[42]

Industry spokesmen have generated a great deal of confusion regarding the level of food chain profits by diverting attention away from profits as a percentage of stockholder equity and directing it instead to profits as a percentage of sales. The latter ratio is low in food retailing because of the relatively thin layer of capital and other inputs provided by food retailers compared with firms in other industries.[43] The level of the profit-to-sales percentage referred to by these spokesmen as typical for food chains is "a little more than one cent per dollar sales." They imply that an industry earning so low a profit rate must be highly competitive. When economists point out that profit/sales ratios are inapplicable for interindustry comparisons, food chain spokesmen say that the ratio has relevance in that it represents the maximum amount that food chains as a group could cut prices without taking losses. Since the ratio is in the range of one percent on sales, food chains could not be responsible for high food prices, according to industry spokesmen.

This justification is subject to question. First, the figure of one to one-and-a-half cents per dollar of sales quoted by food chain spokesmen is a ratio computed after income taxes are substracted. The amount that prices could be cut, assuming no change in costs, would be the before-tax ratio of profits to sales, which, for most large chains, has averaged about 3 percent of sales.

The second problem concerns the use of national averages. Grocery retailing markets are local, levels of profits vary considerably from market to market, companies in some markets earning profit rates significantly higher than the national average of all markets. Data in Tables 10 and 11 indicate that company profitability is significantly related to market position. Profitable markets have a large market share, and unprofitable markets have a small market share. In fact, available data show that large chains typically lose money in small market-share markets and subsidize these operations with high profits earned in large market-share markets. (See, for example, the decision in *In the Matter of National Tea*, FTC docket 7457.)

The total amount of subsidy by large chains currently ranges between a quarter billion to a billion dollars depending on the assumptions used in making the estimate. If the nine chains selected by the staff of the National Commission on Food Marketing in its 1966 study of grocery retailing[44] are a representative of the subsidization activities of all large U.S. food chains, it is possible by means of rather simple calculations to compute an estimate of the dollar amount by which large food chains subsidize their operations in low market-share areas. The amount for the year 1974, conservatively estimated, is over a quarter of a billion dollars (Table 11). A less conservative estimate based on 1975 or 1976 grocery store sales would be closer to $1 billion. If indeed, even the minimum estimate is anywhere near correct, it is not surprising that independent food retailers with small market shares, operating in only one market, and competing against these subsidies, are disappearing in large numbers. Nor is it surprising that in metropolitan areas the concentration of grocery store sales in large food chains is increasing. If large food chains would discontinue subsidizing low market-share markets, prices and profits in the remaining areas could be lower and still achieve the same average. In sum, the amount by which food chains could cut prices, particularly in concentrated food markets, without *losing money* (and assuming no change in costs) is probably several times the one to one-and-a-half percent suggested by industry spokesmen.

In addition to the understatement of the level of profits as a percentage of sales, particularly in concentrated markets, there is an even more significant error which results from using this after-tax profits/sales ratio as a proxy for how much prices could be reduced—namely, failure to account for the fact that the outbreak of competition that would lower prices would also result in re-duced costs. Usually the first costs cut when price competition breaks out in a market are those associated with nonprice forms of company rivalry. A Federal Trade Commission staff study of the Washington, D.C., metropolitan area market indicated that a 1970 outbreak of discounting led to a reduction in prices of more than 3 percent but that cost reductions allowed the food chains to maintain profit rates close to the previous levels.[45] Records which show profit rates earned following the break up of price conspir-acies quite commonly show prices falling several times the profit-to-sales levels existing during the conspiracies. The drop occurs because excess capacity and other inefficiencies, to maintain the conspiracies, were eliminated. We are reminded again of Adam Smith's admonition that monopoly is a great enemy to good man-agement. In food retailing, a Canadian study placed the cost of excess capacity or overstoring in the range of 4 percent of sales. This high level is particularly significant in the light of the recent sharp decline of sales per square foot of floor space in grocery retailing in the United States.

Conclusion

The frequency of high market concentration in both food manufacturing and food retailing is cause for serious concern. There is no reason to believe that the upward trend in both areas is not likely to continue sustained by a combination of factors which increasingly frustrate consumer choice and blunt the forces of competition. In food manufacturing, these factors include:

1. The consumer's increasing real income and the employment of women outside the home. Both have made it not worth while to hunt for in-formation to save small amounts on individual item purchases.

2. Increasing numbers of products among which consumers must choose. This proliferation is caused by technological developments, a demand for new types of products resulting from higher consumer incomes, a change in consumer tastes in favor of more highly prepared foods, and, most importantly, the desire of food manufacturers to differentiate their outputs. The average number of products in grocery stores increased from about 4,000 at the end of World War II to about 10,000 today. The proliferation was accompanied by a replacement of simple products by more complex products, further increasing consumers' need for information.

3. Increased expenditures for food advertising which is aimed at building brand identification and consumer preference for brands rather than providing useful information.

4. A continued merger trend which contributes importantly to the disappearance of medium-sized companies. Many of the acquiring firms are potential competitors in the area of the acquired firms.

Because of these factors, competition in food manufacturing is increasingly controlled by a few large corporations whose special expertise is in creating new product variations, advertising and promoting them, and using field sales personnel to see that their new product variations get favorable treatment on grocers' shelves.

To counter this trend: (1) more convenient and useful information about food products is needed by the consumer; (2) increasing attention should be placed on regulating for both the content and the amount of advertising; (3) mergers which consolidate positions of market power in a few large grocery products corporations should be carefully regulated; (4) in those food product areas where concentration is highest, deconcentration remedies should be pursued by antitrust agencies, or possibly by legislative fiat; (5) a high level of price-fixing surveillance should be made, particularly in local market industries which have a history of being prone to conspiracy.

In grocery retailing, concentration is increasing and already has reached serious proportions in a few of the nation's largest metropolitan areas. High concentration is a frequent problem in smaller cities. Most alarming is the apparently unthwarted upward trend toward more concentration, which appears to derive its thrust in part from market subsidization by large corporate food chains and by the moderately difficult entry conditions in food retailing.

Barriers to new entrants appear to be higher in more concentrated markets and are raised further when established corporate chains use neighborhood price discrimination against the stores of would-be entrants. The rewards of such discriminatory pricing are related to market concentration. Firms holding very large market shares have more to gain from keeping out new competitors. Also, firms with large market shares are more effective in discrimination, because they are likely to have stores in nearly all the neighborhoods which new entrants would enter. A bold antitrust program which would impose heavy penalties on dominant food chains attempting to blockade entry is needed. Such an effort would strongly complement the Federal Trade Commission's current effective regulation of mergers in food retailing.

In addition to improvment of the competitive structure of retail food markets, there is also a need for current, easy-to-use, market basket price information to enable consumers to make effective choices among supermarket chains. With increasing numbers of items to choose from, frequent price changes, confusion caused by price specials, and emphasis on differences in quality and service, the consumer (whose lack of knowledge is increasing because of more frequent moves from one city to another) finds it more and more difficult to make rational choices on the basis of price. As the situation continues to deteriorate, price competition will be further weakened unless outside efforts are made to provide the necessary information.

I endorse the 1966 recommendations made by the National Commission on Food Marketing in its final report, *Food from Farmer to Consumer*, especially its recommendation of financial disclosures and the recommendation that the Federal Trade Commission make an annual report to the President and Congress on competition in the food industries.

Notes

1. *Economic Report of the President*, 1976 (Washington, D.C.: Government Printing Office, 1976), Table B-16, p. 190.

2. Published quarterly in *Marketing and Transportation Situation* [Washington, D.C.: U.S. Department of Agriculture].

3. U.S., Bureau of the Census, *Census of Manufactures, 1972, General Summary* (Washington, D.C.: GPO, 1972), Table 3. The 15.2 percent is not comparable to the 21.7 percent shown on the first page. An important influence making the 15.2 percent lower is that a high proportion of total manufacturing value of shipments reflects producer-good sales.

4. Temporary National Economic Commission, *Large Scale Organization in the Food Industries*, TNEC Monograph 35 (Washington, D.C., 1940).

5. World War II took a heavy toll of food manufacturers with little or no replacement by new entry according to the 1946 Smaller War Plants Corporation report on *Economic Concentration and World War II* (pp. 212-13), which notes that the 25 percent reduction in the number of food processors and manufacturers that occurred between 1939 and 1944 "was due entirely to the elimination of very small food concerns." The heavy demand and high profits earned by food manufacturers in the immediate postwar period permitted introductions of new equipment which had been prevented by war production priorities. This had an uneven effect on individual food industries. The fluid milk industry was hard hit by this, because the new types of machinery and facilities needed to meet upgraded sanitation requirements caused scale economies to increase. Larger processing volumes were needed for efficient utilization of the new processing machinery and milk-handling equipment. During the mid and late 1940s and early 1950s nearly all of the thousands of farmers, producer-distributors, who had processed and distributed their own milk were forced to close their processing operations. See Russell Parker, *Economic Report on the Dairy Industry* (Washington, D.C.: Federal Trade Commission, 1973).

6. *The Census* classifies plants according to whether they had more or fewer than twenty employees.

7. U.S., Bureau of the Census, *Census of Manufactures*, 1972.

8. Joe S. Bain, *Industrial Organization* (New York: John Wiley & Sons, 1959), pp. 124-33.

9. Willard F. Mueller, statement before the Subcommittee on Monopolies and Commerce, Committee on the Judiciary, U.S. House of Representatives, July 19, 1973.

10. U.S., Bureau of the Census, *Concentration Ratios in Manufacturing, 1972 Census of Manufactures*, Table 5.

11. National Commission on Food Marketing, Technical Study No. 8, *The Structure of Food Manufacturing* (Washington, D.C.: By the Commission, 1966), pp. 25, 66, and 221.

12. *Ibid.*, pp. 44, 45. Considering that large food manufacturers tended to occupy high rank positions more than low rank positions (p. 47), positions in concentrated industries more than unconcentrated industries (p. 46), and that there were six unconcentrated or minor industries (ice manufacturing, grease and tallow, animal & marine oils, raw cane processing, rice milling and frozen fish) which they did not participate in at all (p. 49), the percentage of important food industry positions held by the 50 largest was likely to be substantially higher than 70 percent; possibly 80 or 90 percent.

13. *Ibid.*, p. 120.

14. *Ibid.*, pp. 110, 11.

15. *Ibid.*, pp. 126, 127. The number and percentage of leading food manufacturing positions held by large companies increased between 1954 and 1963 (p. 44). The number of leading nonfood manufacturing positions also increased. In total, fifty large food companies held an average of 11.3 of the top four positions in both food and nonfood product classes in 1963. This was a substantial increase from 1954 when each held an average of 9.2 positions (p. 50).

16. *Ibid.*, pp. 125, 126.

17. James S. Worley, "Industrial Research and the New Competition," *Journal of Political Economy*, Apr. 1961.

18. This analysis of performance is limited primarily to prices, costs, and profits. There are other performance characteristics but there are no generally accepted standards for interindustry evaluation. Some of these other dimensions of performance are: variety, convenience, reliability, availability, nutrient content, the composition of food products, safety, sanitation, and consumer information about price, quality, and availability. Many people feel that an equitable distribution of wholesome food to all socioeconomic groups is an important performance characteristic because food is essential to life and at the same time commands a very large proportion of income of the aged and low-to-moderate income families.

19. Adam Smith, *The Wealth of Nations* (1776), Modern Library Edition, p. 147.

20. Bain, *Industrial Organization*, pp. 266-323.

21. National Commission on Food Marketing, *Structure of Food Manufacturing*, p. 71.

22. U.S., Bureau of the Census, *Enterprise Statistics 1967 Part I*, Table 5-1.

23. National Commission on Food Marketing, *Structure of Food Manufacturing*, Table 6-4, and data for subsequent years from *Source Book Statistics of Income*, (Washington, D.C.: Internal Revenue Service).

24. Russell C. Parker, "The Baking Industry," *Antitrust Law and Economics Review*, Summer 1969; and *Economic Report on the Baking Industry* (Washington, D.C.: Federal Trade Commission, 1967), pp. 66-73.

25. Leonard Weiss, "Quantitative Studies in Industrial Organization" in *Frontiers of Quantitative Economics*, ed. by Michael D. Intriligator (Amsterdam: North Holland Publishing Co., 1967). Also, by the same author, "The Concentration-Profits Relationship and Antitrust," in *Industrial Concentration: The New Learning*, ed. by H. J. Goldschmid, H. M. Mann, J. F. Weston (Boston: Little Brown, 1974).

26. Federal Trade Commission, *Economic Report on the Influence of Market Structure on the Profit Performance of Food Manufacturing Companies* (Washington, D.C.: Federal Trade Commission, 1969), p. 7.

27. Federal Trade Commission, *Influence of Market Structure on Profit Performance*, pp. 31-32.

28. B. Imel and P. Helmberger, "Estimation of Structure-Profit Relationships with Application to the Food Processing Section," *American Economic Review*, Sept. 1971, pp. 614-27.

29. Federal Trade Commission, *Economic Report on Food Chain Selling Practices in the District of Columbia and San Francisco* (Washington, D.C.: By the Commission, 1969), p. 4.

30. Federal Trade Commission, *Economic Report on Food Retailing* (Washington, D.C.: By the Commission, 1966), ch. 2.

31. National Commission on Food Marketing, Final Report, *Food from Farmer to Consumer* (Washington, D.C.: By the Commission, 1966), p. 75.

32. Increased services included check cashing, carry out, and increases in service departments such as delicatessens and in-store bakeries.

33. For the decade from 1955 through 1964, which saw the period's greatest increase in gross margins, about 41 percent of the increase was due to trading stamp costs and other promotional expenses. National Commission on Food Marketing, *Food From Farmer to Consumer*, p. 78.

34. The upgrading of physical facilities often included air conditioning and expansion of freezer space, and, in general, of all shelf space to carry a greater variety of products.

35. Ottowa: Queen's Printer, 1968, p. 200.

36. During the period of the most rapid increase in food chain gross margins, 1955 and 1965, large chain gross margins increased 3.5 times as fast as those of small- and medium-sized chains. National Commission on Food Marketing, *Organization and Competition in Food Retailing*, Table 11-2, p. 223.

37. FTC Staff, *Discount Food Pricing in Washington D.C.*, p. 14-17.

38. *Economic Report on Food Chain Profits* (Washington, D.C.: Federal Trade Commission, 1975), p. 11.

39. There was a marked change in the distribution of food retailer profit rates by asset size of company in 1964. This is shown in appendix Figure 1 of the Federal Trade Commission Staff Report on *Food Chain Profits* (1975). Prior to 1964, average profit levels of food retailers were correlated with asset size. From 1964 onward, the correlation disappears. The only significant change that occurred between 1963 and 1964 was a change in the Internal Revenue Service Tax Code eliminating penalties for consolidated reporting of separately incorporated subsidiaries. The geographic divisions of corporate chains are often separately incorporated, although some chains incorporate individual supermarkets.

40. A & P's fortunes during this period were very atypical of other large food chains. While A & P's share of national sales declined from 11 percent in 1958 to about 5 percent in the mid-1970s, the share of the remaining twenty largest U.S. grocery chains increased from 23 percent to 32 percent (Table 7).

41. Federal Trade Commission, *Quarterly Financial Report for Large U. S. Food Chains – Fourth Quarter 1975*, May 3, 1976; also *Food Chain Profits*, Appendix Table 3.

42. See Federal Trade Commission, *Food Chain Profits* for an in-depth analysis of this period, pp. 14 through 20.

43. The ratio of profits to stockholders' equity is the rate of return suggested by economic theory as superior to the ratio of profits to sales as a measure of the economic theory as superior to the ratio of profits to sales as a measure of the economic performance of an industry. Within one industry, different levels of profits-to-sales ratios may indicate comparative company performance, since capital Between industries, however, there are generally wide variations, with grocery retailing being a far outlying observation because of its low capital-to-sales ratio. Because of its low capital-to-sales ratio, the ratio of profits to sales in grocery retailing should be and is low compared with other industries. Food retailing as a stage of production and distribution has very limited functions. Food retailing is a high volume, fast turnover operation. From purchase to sale the average grocery store item stays in the hands of the food chain only a few days. Inventories are held by grocery manufacturers. Low inventory holdings by food retailers substantially reduces the capital costs. The most extensive single function of food retailers is the operation of check-out stands.

44. *Organization and Competition in Food Retailing*, pp. 190-99.

45. *Discounting Food Pricing in Washington, D.C.,* 1971, p. 9 and data submitted to the Joint Economic Committee of the U.S. Congress, 1974. Also see Russell C. Parker, testimony on Washington area food pricing before the District of Columbia City Council in February 1975. The Washington area price reduction was temporary, probably in response to an attempted entry into the area by a new supermarket chain and to an FTC investigation of monopoly in large Washington area food chains underway at the time. The Federal Trade Commission investigation was dropped in the summer of 1973, following which food prices in Washington, returned to their pre-1970 position in relation to those of other cities.

MIND MANAGING THE FOOD AND ENERGY CRISES

HERBERT SCHILLER

The General Crisis

The point of departure for my discussion is the question of how various issues, especially those concerning food and energy, are defined and presented in the media. For a question to receive attention in our society, it must be regarded as a crisis. The attitude seems to be that, if it is not a crisis, why bother? This outlook does not derive from some deep-seated trait in the national character. It is the natural outgrowth of a totally commercialized media system, which prospers when audiences are attracted in large numbers. Accordingly, to obtain large groups of listeners/viewers/readers, it labels almost every situation a crisis, or, at least, a mini-crisis.

Yet the world is filled with *real* crises. No matter where you choose to look, you can discover an authentic crisis. For this reason, it is incumbent on us to explain what constitutes a crisis. Further, who makes the determination? Who defines a situation to make it appear as a crisis?

Let me elaborate. Let us pose some specific questions. Has the United States, and has a significant fraction of the country's population, experienced hunger? Has that been a condition that has existed only in the dim, distant past? Does it apply today? Are there people in this society today who are hungry? I don't think a survey has to be undertaken to supply an answer. Yes! There are large numbers of people in our society who are not receiving a proper nutritional intake. This does not include those who lack a proper diet out of ignorance. Material insufficiency is what is at issue. Yet nobody seems to call this situation a crisis. How is it that it is not viewed as a crisis?

Another example is provided by energy. For decades, American society has been an enormous consumer—I believe that is a generous way of saying a monstrous waster—of energy. Was this or is this a crisis? Few seem to think so. In fact, to question seriously the automobile economy, which uses a good portion of the energy, would be as good a criterion as any for being regarded as an unhealthy deviant. Called into question would be many of the beneficiaries of the entire wasteful infrastructure of supporting activities: motels, shopping centers, highway construction, repair and service stations, and a large number of other automobile-related enterprises.

What, then, is a crisis? A starting point for a definition may be the recognition that those who have some sort of authority, privilege, or benefit to lose, generally are in a position to define what constitutes a crisis. People without authority, without privilege, without standing, voiceless people, who may be undergoing untold miseries—their problems do not receive crisis status.

With this rough rule in mind, let us address the general question of whether or not there are crises in this world, and, additionally, of whether the United States faces crises, and, more specifically, of whether there are energy and food crises.

Larger context

It is more useful, I believe, to begin with the general, larger context. If food and energy fall within a larger category of crisis, as I believe they do, it is important to understand what that larger context is and how, if at all, it is being explained to the national and international community.

Is there an overarching crisis facing us? I find one in the complex of problems associated with Western, industrial capitalism's growth, expansion, and domination during the last several hundred years. This world system, still powerful but now in its declining phase, resists everywhere the efforts of peoples and nation-states to change and reorganize their social and productive methods of existence. This constitutes the central and fundamental crisis of our times. It first appeared after World War I and intensifies from year to year. It permeates economic, political, and cultural life. Indications which support this analysis exist in all spheres.

Take for example, the votes in the United Nations. The United Nations, to begin with, as presented in the American media system, is not anywhere as popular as it was thirty years ago, when the organization was practically an ancillary arm of U.S. foreign policy. Today, votes in the United Nations are often running 100 to 5 or 105 to 1. It is embarrassing to mention who is now in the minority, especially to Americans with world perspectives. It is true that a vote in an international forum does not in itself prove anything. But it should be an indication of something.

Another example: In the last five to ten years there have been many meetings, conferences, and international gatherings. Again, thanks to our informational system, few of us have much recognition of or familiarity with the character of, to say nothing of the participants in, these assemblages. Conferences of the non-aligned countries, Third World enclaves, UNCTAD (United Nations Conference on Trade and Development) meetings have generally been gatherings of 75 to 100 nations, all of whom could be described as poor (some poorer than the rest). Most of the countries participating could be described also as not being able to develop satisfactorily. (The term "developing" nation is avoided because it may be considered a euphemism that doesn't present reality.)

The countries at these meetings and in these organizations have many differences between them. They are not all in the identical situation or condition. But they do share at least one characteristic: they have been suffering exploitation for hundreds of years under the domination of the Western industrial capitalist system. Accordingly, one prong of the general crisis that envelops the Western world comprises the efforts of this large group of nations to change drastically their overall disadvantaged status. These states now challenge, and some of them resist, the long process of domination to which they have been subjected. The United States has by no means been the only participant in their domination, but the United States is the most recent (and perhaps last) dominator; consequently, this country is identified with all the past (and still present) indignities, humiliation, and exploitation.

More significant, in this time of rising resistance, it is the United States which now fights and finances the wars to preserve traditional control arrangements. They are not always called wars. Sometimes they are labeled "police actions" or pacification campaigns or some such. Whatever, the interventions have been numerous over the last few decades: Greece, Korea, Lebanon, The Dominican Republic, Vietnam, Angola, and others less well known.

Where will the next campaign occur? No one knows, but it is safe to say that it will be in one of those many countries comprising the somewhat mysteriously labeled "Third World". In this global sector subsists roughly two-thirds of humanity, mostly nonwhite, the exploited portion of the human race.

To repeat, part of the general crisis that does, in fact, exist is the unwillingness of this vast area of human existence to accept uncomplainingly its current and longstanding impoverished state. The second half of the crisis occurs domestically in the United States (and in a few other developed capitalist nations) where the governing state machinery tries either to meet or to avoid meeting the potential world-wide upheaval.

Media's presentation of crisis

This then, is the crisis, with its international and domestic components. How is this dramatic and historically unique situation presented to the American people? What are they told about these matters? How do the issues appear to the ordinary person? Basically, it is fair to say, I believe, that the contours of this vast drama are obscured if not concealed. Surely they are distorted. When presented at all, the explanation is partial and therefore misleading. A few recent illustrations may be helpful.

What, for example, has been the image of Arabs in the United States in recent years? To raise the question practically supplies the answer. The Arabs have become, in movie terminology, the heavies of the Western world. Those Arabs that appear on American TV screens are shown generally as untrustworthy types, capable of exceedingly ugly behavior. It is not difficult to understand why the Arabs have recently been given this role, held earlier by other scapegoats. If today, the Middle Eastern leaders are shown as holding the world up for ransom as well as causing inflation, there is an explanation. It is not racial, nor is it personal, as much of the domestic imagery suggests. The control and disposition of hundreds of millions of barrels of oil and literally tens of billions of dollars are of no small consequence to American oil companies in particular and to the U.S. corporate economy in general, insofar as systemic needs are concerned.

Turning aside from the Arab image in the United States, consider the informational treatment accorded Soviet society. So far as American presentations go, the Soviets are in the proverbial double bind. They are "losers" whatever they do. In one approach, it is suggested that the Russians can't feed themselves, and, obviously, their entire system must be inoperative. Yet this view creates problems for the Pentagon when it seeks to show congressional appropriating committees that growing Russian power poses an enormous threat to U.S. national security.

One way out of the bind created by arguments that the Russians can't feed themselves and have a totally decrepit society is offered by the suggestion that the Soviets are feeding most of their (and our) grain to livestock. They are being indifferent to world food needs because of their selfish desire for more meat on their own tables. Because meat production entails heavy energy loss (animals walk around as they eat up the grain), aren't the Soviets aware of their wasteful practices?

So, either the Soviet Union is not growing enough grain and the people are starving, or, they are using up scarce grain supplies, feeding it to animals, and eating too many steaks. Of course, it hardly behooves the United States to instruct another society on food conservation practices. And the image of Russians eating meat is not the best item to circulate either after a half-century's Western efforts to demonstrate the inefficiency of socialist organization.

Still another example of message and image control is to be found in the Western capitalist response to the Third World's demands for improved conditions which involve the never totally explicit policy of using food as a weapon. Suggested obliquely, hinted at, mentioned off-hand to reassure the domestic population that our substance will not be squandered on miscreants and ingrates, the idea often lurks behind policy pronouncements. Each defeat suffered (by the United States) in the United Nations produces a renewal of the sentiment, expressed more or less carefully in Washington's bureaucratic corridors and appearing, not so magically, in the daily media.

Domestic components of the crisis

While the resistance of the Third World to imperialism intensifies, a curious but not unpredictable series of developments unfolds domestically. One finds, for example, in the midst of a seeming energy crisis, the oil companies' depletion allowances are extended. The pipe line to Alaska, long postponed by serious reservations concerning its need and impact, is quickly approved. Protection devices against environmental pollution, long battled for, are removed rapidly.

Suddenly, a major campaign is organized to convince the nation that there is a capital shortage. This issue escapes most of the population. In brief, the argument is that huge quantities of capital will be needed to build the facilities and plant that are required to make the country less dependent on off-shore energy supplies. If there is indeed a scarcity of capital, how better to secure additional funds than to allow profits to rise? In capitalist mythology, a 10 percent return (add on a suitable increment for a period of inflation) is supposed to attract capital from the moon. The capital shortage argument, in other words, is the private enterpriser's tried and true gambit to increase profit margins at the expense of the rest of society.

But is is not economics with which we are mainly concerned here. It is, rather, the utilization of message-making and image-creating machinery to persuade the people that the course pursued by the economic power structure is both morally justified and scientifically essential (as indicated by the objective analyses of the rigorous discipline of economics and as befits analysis free of class interest and social bias).

While environmental safeguards are abandoned, depletion allowances extended, and profit margins widened, a remarkable renaissance in cultural programming overtakes the mass media, and television especially. Coincidentally, the patron of the new upsurge of the arts is the oil industry with some assists from companies in other fields. The *New York Times* describes these developments as the appearance of a new Medici.[1] The American equivalent of the Medici clan includes Exxon, Arco, and Mobil Oil. The latest BBC pageant, this cultural spectacular, that artistic event are brought to the nation's viewers at the expense of, and with modest attribution to, the new Medici.

Along with this cultural boom comes the announcement from *Advertising Age*, the organ of the advertising industry, that it has awarded its prize of Advertising Man of the Year in 1975 to someone who happens also to be the chief executive officer of Mobil Oil.[2] Shades of Nero, fiddles, and Rome. As the crisis unfolds on the world stage, the American people, courtesy of the oil industry, one of the big actors in the crisis drama, look at the art treasures of the Western world on TV or listen to a renowned artist perform.

Pressure for change

Outside the home screen, the real crisis deepens as the pressure of the disadvantaged people mounts. The pressure is expressed in many ways but the objective is the same. It is to change the basic economic arrangements of the current world. In recent years this effort has sometimes been referred to as seeking a new international order. Its aim is, simply, to break the stranglehold of the Western industrial system on the rest of the world. As we have noted, this represents the external, or international side of the crisis.

The domestic side is: how does our industrial system react to this pressure, in policy as well as in imagery? Clearly, the imagery is the wrapper, the way the crisis is or is not presented; whether or not it is made understandable so that it can be faced and acted upon by the electorate.

I don't have to remind you to reflect on the number of candidates who sought presidential office this year. How many, if any, of them discussed, however briefly, the Third World, anti-imperialism, multinational corporations, U.S. private investment abroad, U.S. trade and investment patterns, prices and profits, guaranteed employment?

These are unglamorous matters. But they are so regarded only because most of us have been schooled and instructed in ways of thinking that cater to this attitude. The extent to which we find these subjects uninteresting, secondary, unrelated to our personal lives, inaccessible, incomprehensible, is itself an indication of how effectively the process of social control has worked.

To carry the argument further, domestically we find an industrial order that apparently is no longer capable of handling problems which at one time could have been managed in one of at least two ways. One course, the domestic one, could be called the *frontier solution*, the long and continuing pattern in U.S. experience which relied on endless resources. Exhaust one area, one deposit, consume the soil, oil, natural gas, whatever, then move on. In a big country there is always more. But, rich and bountiful as it is, even the United States is not inexhaustible.

When the domestic frontier disappeared, the second boundary was overseas—an international frontier. Copper could be scooped up in Chile and Rhodesia (Zimbabwe). Iron ore could be gouged from Venezuelan mountains. Alumina could be mined in Jamaica. Oil could be drilled in the Persian Gulf. All these resources and many more that are used in Western industrial society were available, at *minimum cost*, from poor societies, too weak to demand their fair share. This is now beginning to come to an end.

As we have already indicated, the contemporary dialogue with the Third World—the traditional hewers of wood and carriers of water—has a new tone. Payment for natural resources and manpower is no longer unilaterally determined by the purchaser. Ten-cents-a-barrel oil (to the oil company purchasers, not to U.S. consumers) is a memory.

The dialogue is not the same everywhere. Exploitation persists. The purchaser hasn't been overcome in many bargaining relationships. Where new conditions have been imposed, they may be reversed, *temporarily*, even by force of arms. Recall the trial balloon that was sent aloft some months ago in the United States. Then, someone wrote an article for one of the "quality" journals, calling attention to those inviting beaches along the Persian Gulf. It offered a great deal of pertinent geographical information. The marvelous sandy beaches, suitable for receiving invasion barges, were not deformed by trees or other foliage suitable for concealment; the area could not become another Vietnam. The locals couldn't hide behind bushes; there are no bushes.

Maybe this was merely a fanciful scenario, a science fiction concoction, or, at worst, an academic adding another publication to his *vitae*. Sometimes, though, such imaginative tales have to be taken seriously. The point is that we don't know whether to ignore or to react to such proposals, because we don't have much input into the decision-making process.

Are military options viable in the contemporary world? Vietnam is still fresh in some people's minds. Can the international side of the crisis, the arousal of the Third World, be handled militarily? Let us turn to high authority for an answer. Mr. Henry Kissenger stressed that Soviet power grew so great in recent decades that the United States cannot dominate international affairs as it once did in the immediate post-World War II period. He added that there was no way to restore our former power position.[3]

What was the Secretary of State actually saying? In truth, it is as close to a direct admission as could be made without explicitly stating it as such, that the United States dominated the world prior to the rise of Soviet power. Contrary to the legend widely propagated in our media in the 1940s and 1950s that the United States was being pushed around by an aggressive Soviet Union, we are *now* being informed that *we can no longer dominate*. Dominating is quite different from being bullied. In fact, it is the embodiment of bullying. So our chief of foreign policy is now complaining that we can no longer bully as we have been accustomed to do.

The American Crisis

Actually, this is, I believe, an accurate reading of reality. American capitalism is blocked from dominating the world but not only because of the Soviet Union. There are, in addition, countries, many of them in the Third World, who are making it very difficult to maintain the old forms of economic and political and cultural domination. Consequently, America is forced back on itself. If the rest of the world will no longer serve as a reservoir and depot, the United States is compelled to rely on its own resources and the functioning of its own economy. And therein rests the source of the crisis now facing the economy. Can the domestic social and economic system operate and meet the needs of its people, under conditions far different from those which have confronted it before?

In framing an answer to this far-reaching question, Barry Commoner's book, *The Closing Circle*, is indispensable. Commoner is writing about pollution and technology and the dimensions of the American crisis. He states:

> The crucial link between pollution and profits appears to be modern technology, which is both the main source of recent increases in productivity and therefore of profits, and of recent assaults on the environment. Driven by an inherent tendency to maximize profits, modern private enterprise has seized upon those massive technological innovations that promise to gratify this need, usually unaware that these same innovations are often instruments of environmental destruction.[4]

This, in brief, is the domestic problem. At the same time the old international control techniques are less and less available—though no time frame can be put around these developments.

Domestically, the economic system is a producer of crises -- environmental, production, and employment. These crises are endemic to the economic system, although, for a variety of reasons, the latter two have been latent for thirty years. It now seems that the special conditions of the last three decades have been exhausted and the return of the business cycle is upon us. It should become increasingly apparent that the economy is unable to function without causing, periodically, both environmental fallout and industrial shutdown and stagnation.

Role of U.S. media

How will these grim developments be explained to us through our informational system? In truth, the informational factor constitutes an additional ingredient in the general crisis. Most of us are unable to comprehend the full dimensions of what is happening (or not happening) in the economy, because the media are unable, *actually institutionally incapable*, of presenting the true character of what is occurring domestically and internationally.

Why? In a word, because the structure of the media is indistinguishable from that of industry. Industry works according to the imperatives of profitability. It introduces technology (or suppresses it), with no heed to social costs. The media operate similarly, except that the pollution from media outputs, which affects the mind, is, if possible, more deadly than the fallout in the physical sphere. Media pollution produces a generalized inability to discern what is occurring in the world.

What is the operational situation? What are some of the component parts of media contamination? Fragmentation of information and the inability (or unwillingness) to present a cumulative historical context for events are two. There are also the withholding of information, the refusal to permit another perspective, and the denial of the opportunity to discover or invent alternative options. Media contamination involves a continuous attack on alternate social arrangements—applicable or not. In the climate it produces, serious social alternatives are viewed, invariably, as unthinkable, and, what is probably worse, most often they are also unmentionable.

In short, the media system obscures the fundamental industrial crisis while the crisis is intensified by the rising challenge of the Third World. This then, is the shape of the crisis of Western capitalism in the last quarter of the twentieth century. Food and energy are very important matters, but they are still only sub-sets in the general crisis.

Projections

Is there a way out? Clearly, the space of a brief discussion hardly allows for ultimate solutions, nor does the enormity of the crisis lend itself to patent prescriptions. The most one can say is that fundamental structural changes will be required internationally and domestically. *Internationally, they will be required and they will be made.* Besides, the United States, as was not the case in the past, will not have the capacity or the strength to prevent these changes. The last few years have already given us some faint indications of what those changes are likely to be. Vietnam provides one instance, Cambodia another, Angola a third. How many more will occur in the years ahead, when they will come, where they will happen, cannot possibly be predicted. But come they will.

In the meantime, in the United States, the media inform us of "miracles." Brazil is considered, in our media, as a "miracle" of development. It has received much publicity. In Brazil, a small fraction of the population is growing wealthy and a large fraction of the community is becoming increasingly impoverished. This kind of a miracle will lead to still greater miracles in the years ahead. Similar developments can be found in several other places under continuing Western tutelage and domination.

Inevitably, these areas will undergo *meaningful* changes. When that time occurs, there will be alarms. The Western media system will identify these developments as crises, menacing to American national security.

Probably, and unfortunately, the people in the United States will be gulled, as they have been so many times in the past. But as the crises multiply, the deception will be less and less successful. It is very difficult to "cry wolf" several times in *one* generation. Far-reaching mass deception, practiced frequently over a short interval, poses problems to manipulators.

Domestically, what is required, more than anything else, is popular awareness about the problems that are being precipitated in the industrial sphere. This, of course, necessitates information of an entirely different sort from what we are accustomed to receiving. A little may trickle through conventional channels, because reality cannot be totally ignored. Events and social phenomena cannot be completely concealed. Some information comes through. However, the size of the crises ahead and their intensity are going to compel the establishment of new channels. Additionally, they are going to propel larger numbers of individuals into the realm of political awareness and action. National perspectives will be affected, and the communications flow will be genuinely two-way for the first time. This development may be a relatively long time in arriving. At this point it is fruitless to become overly concerned with how the structural changes will occur.

Until these major changes come about, what we are likely to experience is a continuation of false crises, crises defined by those who find their benefits and privilege and power threatened. These crises can not overcome, therefore, the underlying sources of the social disorder, which can only worsen. Eventually those whose situations are actually being adversely affected will define the crisis. In this complex and continuously shifting situation, the prospects and the likelihood of change are very great. The underlying conditions are anything but stable. The tempo and the character of the change, when it does occur, are subjects that fall outside this discussion.

Notes

1. John Brooks, "Fueling the Arts, or, Exxon as a Medici," *New York Times*, Jan. 25, 1976.

2. John J. O'Connor, "Mobil's Rawleigh Warner is Adman of the Year," *Advertising Age*, Dec. 29, 1976.

3. *Wall Street Journal*, Feb. 4, 1976.

4. Barry Commoner, *The Closing Circle* (New York: Bantam, 1972), pp. 266-67.

BIOECONOMICS: A NEW LOOK AT THE NATURE OF ECONOMIC ACTIVITY

NICHOLAS GEORGESCU-ROEGEN

I propose to show that the economic process is only an extension of biological evolution and, hence, the most important economic issues must be considered from this entirely new viewpoint. One significant consequence of this evolutionary extension is the dependence of our species on some very scarce resources of matter and energy which exist only in the bowels of the earth. Only humans struggle and fight among themselves over the access to and control of these particular resources. A second important and wholly surprising consequence is the perennial inequalities between social classes within one and the same society as well as between different societies. The same evolutionary extension, not the causes generally assumed by standard economics, is mainly responsible for these inequalities.

It is imperative that economists recognize the crucial role of terrestrial natural resources in the economic process and understand the reasons behind economic inequalities, if the economic problems and dwindling supply of resources which have become evident in the last decades are to be viewed in the right perspective. The solutions derived from this perspective will tell us what we need to do. Even though some of them may be hard to implement, at least they will not lead our efforts astray.

Note: This paper was completed while the author held an Earhart Foundation fellowship. Many of the ideas presented in the paper are part of a book by the author, entitled *Bioeconomics*, to be published by Princeton University Press in 1977, copyright © by Nicholas Georgescu-Roegen.

Biological Evolution and Economic Development

Let us begin by looking at some simple facts. First, mankind is a biological species and, hence, subject to all known biological laws. As the consummate biologist J. B. S. Haldane once reminded us, mankind is subject to extinction, too. At this time, we can only wonder what evolutionary factor will bring it about years from now. The hope—implicit in many environmental arguments— that the human species is immortal (only the individual is mortal) is not supported by factual evidence. But even though we are a biological species, we are a unique one. Some biologists and, following them, a host of others have argued that we are distinguished from the rest of the living creatures by the superiority of our biological nature. Haldane, again, pointed out that this position reflects man's desire to pat himself on the back and wittily added that, to a monkey, "the change from monkey to man may very well seem a change for the worse."[1]

What makes our species unique is its extraordinary mode of evolving. All species, including ours, have progressed by biological mutations which gradually endow the living individuals with stronger muscles, sharper claws, sharper eyes, and so forth. The rub is that this way of improving the life of a species requires a tremendously long time. During the Eocene era, there existed an animal—paleontologists now call it *Eohippus*—which was no bigger than a beagle. By successive biological mutations it took that small animal fifty million years to become the powerful horse which now can easily pull a plow or win the Derby. The salient characteristic of the human species is that it did not wait for immensely slow biological evolution to enable it to perform actions that no other species can. Man can now run faster than the cheetah, pull greater weights than the elephant, and fly faster and higher than any bird. This result has been achieved rather simply.

The origin of the process goes back twenty million years to a primeval ancestor of ours, the *Proconsul*. Repeated experiences with a club picked up accidentally from the woods eventually must have led the members of that species to feel that with a club an arm becomes longer and more powerful. The *Proconsul* thus began habitually carrying a club, just as if the club had been as integral a part of its body as its arm. When *Homo sapiens* e-merged, he thus emerged as an animal that used detachable limbs—i.e., limbs which are not part of the body (soma) with which each individual is endowed by birth but which are, rather, produced and used as needed. Following Alfred J. Lotka, we may refer to these as *exosomatic* organs and to those which belong to the body as *endosomatic*.[2] The important point is that both kinds of organ serve in essentially the same way. One may walk to school or ride a bicycle. And an intelligent being from another world may very well see no difference between the knife that cuts the bread and the hand that guides the knife.

It is through producing increasingly more powerful, sharper, speedier detachable limbs that the human species has become what we are today and what we will be in the future. Economic development is nothing but extension of the biological evolution. But we should not fail to note that the exosomatic evolution was made possible only because of a parallel biological evolution of the human brain. The two actually form a dialectical tandem, which is one of the reasons why the nature of the exosomatic evolution is so akin to biology. "The Mecca of the economist lies in biology rather than economic dynamics," warned Alfred Marshall.[3]

The two evolutions indeed have much in common. To the mutations of the biological evolution there correspond the exo-somatic innovations. Both also seem to occur without any regularity, not even with the dialectical, irregular regularity which characterizes randomness.[4] Nowadays, we seek to increase the emergence of innovations through Research and Development (R&D), but innovations seem to escape any predictive system. And just as we do not know, for example, exactly where, when, and in what individuals the eye appeared first, we also do not know who invented, say, the wheel or the canoe. Nor is it true that mutations or innovations are the product of want, need, or necessity. To think it true would be a return to Lamarckism, to the idea that the giraffe came about because of the need to reach the leaves on tall trees. There still are numberless important human wants which are not satisfied. The fact that no innovation is adopted unless it satisfies some want (however irrational or flimsy) should not cause us to reverse the association between the two articulations.

Both innovations and mutations are qualitative, not quantitative, changes. The difference was marvelously explicated by a short parable of Joseph A. Schumpeter, who is the only economist to analyze economic development in a manner completely homomorphic with the traditional analysis of evolutionary biology. "Add successively as many mail coaches as you please," he said, "you will never get a railway thereby."[5] A biologist may aptly echo the idea by saying "Add as many gills as you please, you will not get a lung thereby."

Like mutations, innovations compete with each other under the rule of the natural selection of the fittest. Innovations also spread through a diffusion process similar to that encountered in the biological domain. First, for an innovation to pass from one group to another, there must be some intimate contact. Second, and more important, the adopting group must also be potentially receptive.

Finally, innovations are inheritable, not more and not less than mutations. Mutations are transmitted by genetic inheritance, which ensures the continuation of the biological life of a species (to some very large, yet finite, extent). A human can certainly learn by himself how to use his endosomatic organs—the legs for walking, the hand for grasping, and so on. But no human—except the innovator himself—can pilot a jet plane or even carve a bow without training. Another characteristic feature of the human species determines the use of the prevailing exosomatic organs in continuation—namely, tradition. Its role is that of exosomatic heredity.

Tradition is the essence of what anthropologists call culture. It emerged naturally with the use of the earliest rudiments of exosomatic organs. Tradition gradually came to include instructions, not only of a purely technical nature, but also precepts or rules of social behavior. It has become increasingly more complex, and perhaps even more mythological, as the exosomatic structure itself has grown in complexity; witness both the different rationalizations of the present social and political setups in the various countries of the world and the intractability of the associated legal scaffolds.

Production: Source of social conflict

What are the momentous by-products of the exosomatic evolution, which we mentioned at the start of this essay?

At the dawn of their existence as a distinct species, humans lived in amorphous, dissociable packs. The gregarious instinct, as Thornstein Veblen taught us, brought people together. The pack or herd offered the Darwinian advantages of sexual intercourse adapted to the human constitution and of better defense. But at the dawn of history, the exosomatic organs were simple— a club, a slingshot, or a bow and arrow, for example. These could be made by one individual, at most by the cooperation of a few members of the same family. Gradually, however, exosomatic organs became more complex, so that their production required the cooperation of a far greater number of hands. Production then had to become a social undertaking, which compelled the human communities to organize themselves in *societies*.

By its very nature, social production requires two kinds of roles: Some individuals must plan, supervise, and control the process of production; others must only perform tasks assigned to them. In Adam Smith's terminology, the former represents unproductive, the latter productive labor.[6] However, the division with its roots in production passed into a social precipitate: the division between the governing and the governed classes, as we find it in absolutely every community involved in social production, whatever its political setup might be.

Both types of labor are, no doubt, useful and necessary. The drawback of the division is that it gives rise to the social conflict which has plagued all human societies. And, given what we know about human nature as well as the evolution of other species, the human species very likely would rather die in penthouses than return to a primitive form of life requiring no social production. Be this as it may, the social conflict will continue to plague mankind as long as it relies on a complex exosomatic existence.

Because the exosomatic, in contrast to the endosomatic, organs do not by nature belong to any particular person who performs some labor within the society, the issue of who shall enjoy their services becomes intertwined with the issue of what kind of work one shall perform. Who shall go down the mine shaft and who shall eat caviar and drink champagne? This is the big question. In view of the nature of the root of the social conflict, no social scheme could possibly eliminate the social and economic differences between the "governors" and the "governed." What we can hope (and strive hard) to do is to prevent this difference from becoming abusively great.[7] As social scientists, we would betray our professed ideals if, instead of recognizing this fact overtly, we would continue to delude the people, who look to us for guidance, into believing that one or another fetish scheme can bring about a social New Jerusalem.

A counter-proof that social conflict is the product of the exosomatic evolution is supplied by other social species—bees, ants, and termites, in particular, who also live in organized and sufficiently complex societies but have reached that stage through endosomatic, not exosomatic, evolution. The crucial difference is that in insect societies each individual is fit by birth for a specific task. For example, a doorkeeper in an ant colony is born with a flat head, with which it blocks the entrance to the hill, opening it only to the recognized members. Moreover, the doorkeeper does not like to do anything other than this particular job. There is therefore no reason for a conflict between the various classes of individuals. When, as the winter approaches, the bee workers kill most of the drones, it is not a civil war, but a normal biological phenomenon; the drones are already overcome by a naturally produced stupor.

Things are different within human society. No one is biologically destined at birth for any particular occupation. Later in life, one can become a rickshaw man as well as a mandarin. Also, my human, in contrast with a member of an insect society, would certainly prefer to be a mandarin rather than a rickshaw man, a president of a corporation rather than a janitor, a commissar rather than a kolkhoz hand. What one will ultimately be is in great part the result of the social forces operating in one's own society.[8]

Intersocial inequality

Besides inequality within one and the same society, the exosomatic evolution is also responsible for intersocial inequality. The human species has been divided (and still is) into several biological races. Like all biological races, human races can operate biologically with each other perfectly well. Conceivably, one couple of any two different races is capable of perpetuating alone the human species. But, for reasons still difficult to ascertain because nothing comes near to controlled experiment in this field, mankind has also been divided into different exosomatic species. I say "species" in this case, because the groups are as differentiated exosomatically as the ordinary cat (*Felis domestica*) is biologically differentiated from the cougar (*Felis concolor*), perhaps even more differentiated.

At the time when the Pharaohs were able to build the pyramids, the people of Central Europe were living at the exosomatic level of the Cro-Magnon man. Even greater differences exist today. Compare the rudimentary tools used by the Upper Amazonian tribes with the industrial leviathan of the United States. Even *Homo Indicus* is exosomatically different from *Homo Americanus*, in spite of the former's ancient and once splendid culture. The exosomatic level of the *Homo Americanus* is epitomized by the electric range, preferably with a self-starting, self-stopping, and self-cleaning oven. The corresponding tool in the Asian subcontinent is a primitive cooking contraption in which dried dung is burned.[9] Exosomatic differences such as these are the basic reason why immense financial support from the United States and recently also by other Western nations failed to develop the underdeveloped economies. Because of the qualitative exosomatic differences between the developed and the undeveloped nations, no exosomatic organ can be transplanted from the former to the latter. Financial aid from the United States was completely successful in helping put the developed countries devastated by World War II—from Norway to Greece and Japan—back on their feet, precisely because all these countries had the same exosomatic structure as the United States.

The exosomatic level of the Western nations cannot possibly offer any substantial help to India, for instance. In the United States the current R&D is directed toward construction of a "thinking oven," because for the U.S. people nothing else would do. How could R&D with such an orientation possibly help the Indians to improve their mode of cooking, of transportation, and so on? Actually—and this is much more saddening—even in India the R&D is not preoccupied with how to improve the prevailing exosomatic situation there.

Clearly, substantial exosomatic inequalities cannot be eliminated by simple financial aid alone, no matter how generous. Only research at the low level of the underdeveloped countries can help. But such a project implies long and widespread field work for which even a Peace Corps would not suffice. As I argued some ten years ago, what is needed is a Peace Army.[10] Without this, the gulf between the developed and the undeveloped will in all probability increase instead of becoming smaller. The difficulty with this plan is that a Peace Army presupposes a kind of generosity entirely different from that on which simple financial or technical aid leans. It may be described only as the greatest possible generosity. Perhaps mankind may not be capable of this turn of heart. But this possibility should not cause us to ignore the fact that, as is not the case with the inequality between social classes, there is no reason to prevent the elimination of the inequalities between different societies. In the very long and terribly hard run, the inequalities may disappear whether we will do something about them or not.

Role of Natural Resources in the Economic Process

View of standard economics

All living creatures struggle over the means of survival. We are no exception. But the other creatures need only solar energy and some chemical substances from the topsoil, the air, and the waters. Because our exosomatic organs are ordinarily produced from and with the aid of mineral resources, man had to become a geological agent, the only such agent among all species. The control over mineral resources has always provided the driving force of all great historical commotions, whether wars or migrations. The reason is that a simple test of time convinced most people that all resources are consumed, as it were, through use, even though it took science a very long time before incorporating this truth into its official records.

In spite of this plain evidence, standard economics preferred to ignore the absolutely crucial role natural resources played in the economic process. Natural resources are simply given no place in the standard analytical considerations.[11] This fact is justifiable to some extent and, at the same time, greatly curious. At the time when standard economics was born, natural resources seemed to exist in virtually unlimited supply (which may very well have been why Karl Marx, too, denied any role in the economic process to natural resources). The Neoclassical forefathers wanted to build a new economics after the model of mechanics because the records of mechanics were still glowing brightly. Had not Urbain Leverrier discovered the planet Neptune in 1846, not by scanning the firmament, but at the tip of his pencil after some paper-and-pencil manipulation of the equations of mechanics? The curious thing is that at the time when standard economics began its career, the merchanistic epistemology had already fallen from favor in physics itself. But it is most curious of all that economic science has never tried to break away from the grips of the mechanistic dogma.[12]

Anyone who thumbs through any of the most respected economic manuals, would easily come across the ultrafamiliar diagram by which standard economics portrays the economic process (Figure 1). This view of the economic process as a self-sustaining

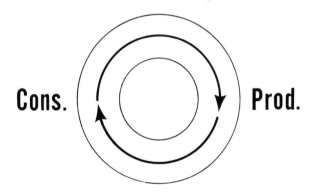

Fig. 1. Economic process as portrayed by standard economics.

merry-go-round between production and consumption, or (mark the point) just as well between consumption and production, is the most vexing symptom of the mechanistic epistemology. It may also reflect the business viewpoint, which reduces that process to the circulation of money. (But even monetary signs cannot last forever.)

The economic process is not a mechanics of self-interest and utility, although these factors provide some of the driving forces. The sad state of standard economics derives from the fact that the economic process is solidly anchored in the material environment and, moreover, what happens in this environment cannot be portrayed as a mechanical pendulum. What happens from the viewpoint of life phenomena in the environment, in the entire universe, is subject to the laws, not of mechanics, but of thermodynamics.

Applicability of the laws of thermodynamics

Thermodynamics as a rule, seems a simple science. Yet its analytical framework is studded with highly intricate concepts and issues. For the purposes of a general analysis of the economic process, a simple plastic representation will do.

I propose to represent an isolated system—such as the whole universe, for example—by an hourglass (Figure 2). The stuff

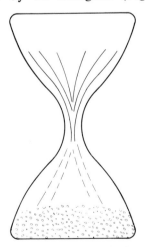

Fig. 2. Matter-energy in an isolated system.

inside it represents matter-energy. And, since the hourglass is completely sealed, the constancy of the amount of the stuff reflects the First Law of Thermodynamics, the Law of Conservation of Matter-Energy. As in any hourglass, the stuff continuously pours from the upper half down into the lower one. Two facts distinguish the hourglass of the universe from an ordinary glass.

First, whereas the amount of matter-energy remains constant, the quality of matter-energy changes. As long as matter-energy remains in the upper half, it is in a state in which it can be used by us humans as well as by any form of terrestrial life. This valuable quality is gone as soon as matter-energy falls into the lower half. The first state constitutes *available* matter-energy, the second *unavailable* matter-energy. Because this distinction has an anthropomorphic basis, purists place thermodynamics into a category by itself, separate from physics. The truth is that thermodynamics is the physics of economic value—the reason why all economists should be well acquainted with its teachings.[13]

The second peculiarity of the hourglass of the universe is that it cannot be turned upside down. This means that available matter-energy is continuously and *irrevocably* degraded into the unavailable form. If we now note that the highly intricate concept of entropy is, at bottom, an index of the relative level of the unavailable matter-energy, the last statement is equivalent to the Entropy Law. In a form more explicit than that ordinarily found in the literature, it can be stated as follows: *The entropy of an isolated system continuously and irrevocably tends toward a maximum which occurs when the system ultimately reaches thermodynamic equilibrium (and contains no more internal available matter-energy).*

One particular point in connection with this law needs to be clearly emphasized. Not only energy (as is generally believed by the host of tyros now attracted by the topical issues of resource scarcity), but also matter, continuously and irrevocably dissipates. All around us matter is continuously oxidized, chipped, cracked, washed or blown away, and so on. But surprising though it may seem, even the academic literature errs on this point. The first thing mentioned in all elementary textbooks on thermodynamics is the transformation of work into heat by friction. But no manual, to my knowledge, takes into account the fact that friction dissipates matter as well. At times, the argument against the irrevocable entropic degradation of matter alludes to the possibility of reassembling the parts of a whole. True, if the pearls of a broken necklace scatter over the floor of a large auditorium, we can reassemble them—but only at the cost of a substantial amount of energy, of some additional matter, and, above all, of some appreciable time. It would be, however, utterly inept to extrapolate this fable to the case in which the pearls are first dissolved into some acid and the solution sprinkled over the oceans. It is obvious that the length of time necessary for reassembling these pearls would be practically infinite. This requirement alone makes the operation unrealizable in actuality.[14] In this connection, one may recall that the consecrated theory teaches that, if one could move a thermodynamic system with infinitely small speed, one could reverse any change. The impossibility of reversible changes and of reassembling unavailable matter thus stems from one and the same reason: the infinite time required to achieve them.[15]

Another point worthy of emphasis is that matter-energy degrades regardless of whether or not life is present. A pile of coal, left by itself, "sweats"; it becomes wet as the chemical energy of the coal is gradually transformed into water, carbon dioxide, and dissipated heat. Or the whole pile of coal can catch fire via spontaneous combustion.

The Entropy Law is the only natural law for which the presence of life matters. Some forms of life—the green plants, especially— slow down the degradation, while the so-called consumers—animals, bacteria, etc.—speed it up. These facts do *not* violate the Entropy Law, because this law does not specify the speed of degradation with respect to mechanical time, to which we relate any measure of speed. In other words, there is an entropic indetermination in the material world which is responsible for many still poorly understood life phenomena.[16]

The Entropy Law teaches in the form of denials; we cannot use the exhaust fumes from an automobile to drive an engine, nor can we reassemble into a new tire the rubber molecules spread over the road surfaces from a worn out tire. We can use *a given amount of low entropy*—whether energy or matter—only once.[17]

We certainly can recycle matter, but not *dissipated* matter. We can recycle only matter that is still available but no longer in a shape useful to us; this is "garbojunk"—broken bottles, worn out motors, old newspapers, and the like.[18] The Entropy Law is the taproot of economic scarcity. In a world in which this law did not apply, the energy of a piece of coal could be completely converted into work, the work again into energy, and so on endlessly. Tools also would not wear out. But life would not exist either. It would be foolish, therefore, to wish that the Entropy Law (implicitly, scarcity) did not apply.

The earth as a closed entropic system

The entropic nature of the economic process in its relation with the accessible environment may be plastically represented by a slight modification of our earlier hourglass (Figure 2). In the new representation, a coiled tube stands for the economic process, which takes available matter-energy from the surroundings and, after using it, expels it in the unavailable form into the same environment (Figure 3). An input flow of valuable resources

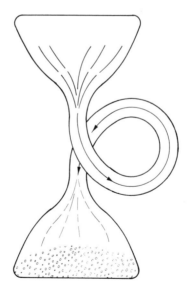

Fig. 3. Relation of economic process and accessible environment in an open thermodynamic system.

enters the process and an output flow of what goes by the general name of "waste," valueless from the economic viewpoint, comes out. At all times some matter-energy is passing through, or rather is being used within, the system; in the very apt term of Kenneth E. Boulding it is the *throughput*.[19] We must however note that, unless we take a very long view of the happenings, the economic system has a material scaffold of quasi-enduring funds. These are the agents of the process—the people, the tools in general, and, to be sure, the land.[20] The fundamental role of the throughput is to keep people and tools in working condition. I say "tools" as well because for an exosomatic existence their maintenance is as vital for the people as the maintenance of the endosomatic organs. Just imagine, if anyone can, what would happen if, by some supernatural legerdemain, all exosomatic instruments were destroyed at once.

Unquestionably the economic system must contain a material scaffold, because we cannot manipulate energy without the aid of a material contraption. Except in a few instances—such as the photon—energy completely separated from matter does not exist even at the subatomic level. At that level, however, there are phenomena for which the Einsteinian evidence $E = mc^2$ applies. But in actuality not all is as simple as it looks on paper.

The Einsteinian equivalence ordinarily works in the conversion of matter into energy, not vice versa. Even in the greatest accumulations of matter-energy, there is no appreciable formation of matter from energy alone, from scratch. In nuclear reactions we have succeeded in increasing the mass of the uranium atom so as to obtain transuranium elements. But no transformation of pure energy into, say, copper is possible under the conditions of this planet.

There is still another reason why any economic analysis of natural resources must take individual account of both energy and matter.

When terrestrial available matter continues to be accessible, the economic process may be represented by the coil hourglass of Figure 3, with a throughput of both matter and energy. This case corresponds to an *open* thermodynamic system. However, the earth itself is, for all practical purposes, a *closed* system, i.e., a system which exchanges only energy, the input of solar radiation and the output of dissipated thermal energy, outside itself. Its material content always remains the same from the outset. The number of copper atoms that exist today on and inside the earth is the same as when the planet became a relatively stable cosmic body.[21]

A closed system is portrayed by the coiled tube of the hourglass in Figure 4, in which the thick, round arrow represents the constant amount of matter that is whirled around. But since there is no inflow of matter (of any entropic quality), since matter cannot be obtained from energy by conversion, and since dissipated matter cannot be recycled, it is clear that the continuous entropic degradation of matter in a closed system must reach a point at which internal work can be performed no longer. In other words, a closed system cannot be a steady state, except after its material entropy has reached its maximum.[22] In view of this, in the very long run, matter may become the truly crucial scarcity for mankind.[23]

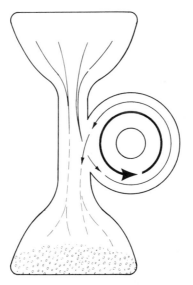

Fig. 4. Matter in a closed thermodynamic system.

This point bears upon the revived form of an idea of John Stuart Mill, which is now expounded and defended most cogently by Herman Daly.[24] The idea undoubtedly has some implicit merits—the highest being its denunication of the mania for growth which the best authorities of standard economics have spread all over the world. But the argument that the ecological salvation of mankind lies in the steady state economy goes against the entropic facts discussed in these pages as well as against the geological structure of the planet. Only struggle, continuous struggle, with a niggardly nature lies ahead in mankind's future. Our highest hope is to attenuate its intensity.

An inventory of our entropic dowry and of our potentialities will help us find the way toward this more modest, but hopefully achievable, goal.

Available and accessible matter-energy sources

It is befitting to begin with the energy of the sun. The sun radiates annually $10^{13}Q$—a fantastic amount, Q itself being an astronomical unit ($Q = 10^{18}$ BTU). Of this amount, the earth intercepts only 5,300 Q per year, i.e., about 100 Q per week. But even this amount should be staggering by our ordinary scales of measurement. For example, according to the most optimistic estimates, the entire stock of fossil fuels amounts to only 200 Q. This amount could provide us with only two weeks of sunlight, whereas the sun will shine with almost the same intensity for at least another 200 billion weeks (4.5 billion years)—certainly, much longer than the probably life-span of the human species.

Solar energy also has the great (and unique) advantage of producing no pollution in the strict sense of the term. Like a waterfall, solar energy ends up in the same form whether it is used or not.[25] It has, however, a tremendous and unique drawback when it comes to being harnessed industrially. Solar energy reaches us as a very fine mist. If it were a rain mist instead of a radiation mist, we might capture its kinetic energy by a large metal plate. The droplets hitting that plate could perhaps crush a city the size of Detroit, provided the plate were large enough—possibly as large as Michigan itself. (Let us not ask now how thick such an immense plate should be and how much it should weigh.) Fortunately, we do not have to capture the rain; the finest mist collects by itself in rivulets, creeks, and rivers. All we need to do is find a place where billions of raindrops have come together to form a waterfall. Solar energy, in sharp contrast with the rain mist, does not accumulate by itself. To catch its finely dispersed energy we need some plate—as great as that just described, if we wanted to obtain an important amount of available energy.[26]

Various schemes for a cheap way to harness solar energy keep coming from the bandwagon of self-styled energy experts. What all these schemes ignore is that the extremely weak intensity of solar radiation cannot possibly be altered. It is a physical constant (the Langley constant), determined by the cosmological structure of our solar system. Nor is it possible to cause solar radiation to concentrate by itself so that we may catch a lot of it with only a small plate. If solar energy is to become the only source in the future, it will have to be through natural processes, in which case, mankind's mode of life will have to be greatly altered. Relying mainly on solar energy necessarily means, in large measure, going back to nature. Urban agglomerations are incompatible with an economy based primarily on solar energy. They are huge entropy-producing machines in any case, for they cause matter to be dissipated over and above the natural entropic process. Think only of the nitrogen, for example, which ends up dissipated in the ocean waters because of the enormous quantity of food eaten in the large cities.

Another alternative open to mankind is nuclear energy. Although the stock of this energy does not amount to much more than that of fossil fuels if it is used in the ordinary reactors, if used in the breeder, it could provide ample energy for a population of twenty billion for perhaps another one million years—some say.[27] But this grand plan is fraught with unforeseen consequences for the human species, perhaps even for the whole of terrestrial life. It represents a truly Faustian deal. The advocates of this technological fix do not tell us how to store the nuclear garbage safely. Nor do they suggest what to do with the mountains of crushed rock resulting from extracting uranium from New Hampshire granite or Chattanooga black shale. It is of still graver concern that only about eight pounds of plutonium-239 suffice to make a simple atom bomb. And there is no way of ensuring that plutonium-239 won't get into hands not controlled by sane minds. Hundreds of pounds of nuclear material are already unaccounted for in the United States alone. Certainly, mankind is at the most fateful crossroad in its history.

The physicists' dream, controlled nuclear reaction (which, though not completely clean, is relatively safe), is still a dream. Hopes that once were sanguine have gradually taken on a skeptical tint.[28] It is not excluded that—as I have ventured to specualte for some time now[29]—thermonuclear energy could elude man's harness forever. Experience with other equally highly intensive engergies—from that of the thunderbolt to that of gunpowder—proves that this idea is not a flight from reality.[30]

However we may turn this dilemma around, one fact is inescapable: mankind's dowry of accessible, available matter-energy is finite. I wish to stress the qualificative "accessible." We are a spaceship floating on a cosmic sea of available matter-energy, but, being limited to only a speck of the cosmic space, we can have access only to an infinitesimal fraction of that available matter-energy. Those who keep on speaking about so-called escape to other solar systems ignore that the closest suns that might possess planets such as ours are about ten light-years away. Just an exploratory journey by a fast space rocket would require at least 200 years! Simple communication by radio signals with other intelligent beings would have to span two successive generations, at best.

The qualification regarding accessibility applies to even terrestrial resources. Certainly there exists matter-energy—such as some shale oil—which is available but inaccessible because it would take a greater amount of low entropy to extract it than that contained in it.[31]

But the difficulty does not end here. Some authors, beginning with Fred Cottrell,[32] have spoken of net energy. The difficulty with this proposal is that we need both matter and energy to get matter or energy. No operation can therefore be performed with only an input of either energy or matter alone. Since matter and energy cannot be reduced to a practical common denominator, we cannot decide on purely physical grounds which of two systems, one using more matter, the other more energy, is more efficient. This decision can be made only via economic considerations, such as the relative accessibility of the resources involved in terms of human effort. For, although the economic process *is* entropic, the roots of economic value are not confined to the physical domain.[33] The old tenet of William Petty, although now forgotten, is the crystal truth: Labor is the father and nature the mother of wealth.[34] But let us mark the point well; ecological value involves considerations other than the economic ones.

Fallacies of Standard Economics

Standard economics has not erred only by completely ignoring the economic role of nature. Its second error has been its refusal to recognize the size of population as a factor in the economic problem. Having embraced from the outset the belief in unlimited growth—the conjuring trick which they dignified with a mathematical armamentarium of exponential functions—standard economists consigned Malthus's doctrine to the lowest disrepute. This is epitomized by Mark Blaug's verdict in the article on Malthus in the *International Encyclopedia of the Social Sciences* (IX, 551): "The Malthus theory of population is a perfect example of metaphysics masquerading as science." One obviously cannot accept Malthus and preach growthmania at the same time.

The truth is that Malthus was not Malthusian enough,[35] for he did not deny that population may grow without limit so long as it did not grow faster than the means of subsistence. This is indeed the essence of his position which he, unfortunately, cast in the much-maligned form: population grows exponentially, the means of subsistence only linearly.

What we should retain as valuable from Malthus is that the size of population puts pressure on the available resources. This problem has been greatly misunderstood, with the consequence that a large literature has grown around the concept of optimal population. Nowadays, some say that the earth could feed even fifty billion people provided that the best available agricultural techniques are applied on all potential plow land. What these authors forget to tell us is how long the earth could maintain such a population. From what we have discussed in the foregoing sections, one should also ask how long a population of even one million could survive. The answers to these questions depend primarily upon what methods are used to grow food.

A mechanized agriculture with high-yield varieties shortens the life-span of any population, regardless of size, because mechanized agriculture with high-yield varieties constitutes, surprising though it may seem, an immense squandering of scarce resources.[36] It substitutes factors that deplete terrestrial resources—tractors, gasoline, chemical fertilizers—for those that depend mainly on solar energy—beasts of burden, manure, and rotation by fallow.[37] We have no better solar cells operating at the ground level than the horse, the ox, or the water buffalo.

We also have been blinded by a third fallacy of standard economics—the absolute belief in the power of technology, in the tenet that any technological innovation can bring lasting progress to mankind. Such a belief is essential to growthmania. Yet technology has, more often than not, moved against the economy of resources. Examples can be supplied at will. But such things as push-button automobiles and photosensitive, automatic flagpoles pale in comparison to mechanized agriculture.

Nevertheless, at this time, we cannot possibly return to organic agriculture, in which man must share the fertile land with his beasts of burden and also get a smaller yield per acre. Such a move is rendered absolutely impossible by the present size of the population—four billion—which, no doubt, exceeds the *organic* carrying capacity of the earth. Furthermore, each year there are now eighty million more people—not all newborns—to be fed. It is as if each year a new West and a new East Germany came into the world. To feed only these additional mouths, the supply of grain must be increased each year by twenty million tons. And the current production cannot suffice to eliminate the malnutrition and starvation of millions.

Implications of the Closed System for Economics

In the light of the ideas developed in the preceding pages, what can an economist propose? Should one join the chorus of standard economists who still preach that, come what may, we shall find a way because technology also grows exponentially? Shall one join them in teaching that the best of worlds is at hand provided the prices are right? Or shall one listen to their professed faith in the power of benefit-cost analysis? I submit that one should do none of these things.

Technology cannot exceed the theoretical limit of efficiency established almost two hundred years ago by the founder of the thermodynamic science, Sadi Carnot. It cannot even reach that level. The only miraculous progress achieved by technology is that of harnessing new types of energy. But here we must weigh the dangers against the benefits. Let us hope that man is not so "rational" as to choose industrial comfort at the cost of dying from nuclear poisoning. As concerns controlled fusion, one should be reminded that there is no wisdom in building houses without staircases and elevators in the hope that technology may one day screen out gravitation. Let us first wait for the miracle.

We cannot possibly rely on the market mechanism to avoid ecological catastrophes, because the market is the parameters of demand and supply only of current generations, whose horizon is just a brief spell in comparison with the life span of the whole species. Prices can never be ecologically right, simply because future generations are not present to bid on the scarce resources side by side with the current generation.[38] If all future generations could also bid, there would probably be no steel available for anything other than plowshares and sickles. Yet we are lavishly producing Cadillacs, Rolls Royces, and Volgas.[39]

Cost-benefit analysis works well when there is a set of perfectly known data and everything has a definite price in money—a situation fitting ordinary problems of business enterprises. But if we turn to ecological problems, there is no price for resources *in situ*, no money cost for removing irreducible pollution, and no price for a human life. In this case, a cost-benefit analysis would look downright silly, even if considered as a paper-and-pencil exercise— as one may convince oneself by perusing the literature recently emanating from no less a source than the National Academy of Sciences.[40]

When supply becomes increasingly shorter than the demand for basic needs, the only sane thing an economist can do—and ought to do—is turn to the most elementary principle of economizing, which is *to act on demand*. This does not mean that all endeavors to find new ways of increasing the supply should be discouraged. It means only that one should not delude people into believing that epoch-making innovations are just around the corner. Project

Independence is indeed the grandest illusion. No nation, not even the entire world, can ever achieve independence. Because—as I have demonstrated earlier—no closed system can be a workable steady state, much less a workable growing state.

To act upon demand certainly implies a change in the scale of values—a feat that has so far been the prerogative of history aided by catastrophes of various natures. Yet, if we do not at least draft a bioeconomic program that follows logically from the facts and articulations presented in this essay, we fail in our mission as scholars; we would allow those who now make the headlines with schemes of entropy bootlegging—tantamount to patching the elbow holes in the sleeves with a bigger piece of cloth cut from the bottom of the pants—to lull the world into a dangerous feeling of security.

A bioeconomic program

At the risk of being branded Utopian (a charge to which I would plead guilty with both pride and humility), by way of conclusion I shall submit an old minimal bioeconomic program of mine.[41]

First, production of all instruments of war must cease completely. It is an unparalleled hypocrisy to outlaw the waging of war while continuing to produce more and more nuclear warheads as amiably agreed at international meetings. The immense amount of resources that go into the production of armaments in the entire world could certainly be put to better uses.

Second, population everywhere, not only in the overpopulated countries, must be slowly brought down to the level which can be sustained by organic agriculture alone.[42] Certainly, the move must affect the overpopulated countries more. Just to get some idea of the dimensions involved, one should try to imagine a United States as densely populated as Bangladesh. It would then have no fewer than five billion people, one billion more than the present world population. Doubts concerning the ability of even U.S. technology to feed such a population are completely in order.

Third, the undeveloped countries must be helped to get rid of hunger and its frightful consequences. Current practice, which is to keep sending food to the hungry, will not do. The poor must be brought to a level at which they can feed themselves. And since the hungry as a rule live in overcrowded countries, nothing short of mechanized agriculture with high-yield varieties will work (at least for some time to come). But mechanized agriculture, in contrast to organic agriculture, is tributary to a well-developed industry. Therefore, the slogan of the day must be "Factories, not food, for the hungry"—factories, not to produce luxury goods (like those built with past aid), but to supply tractors, plows, and fertilizers.

It goes without saying that this program implies not only a Peace Army but also the renunciation by the rich nations of their extravagant mode of life, not to mention the growthmania. Without this change of heart, the inequality between the poor and the rich nations is very likely to increase, as illustrated by the recent evolution of the oil market. Since the financial power of the rich nations can easily absorb practically the entire oil supply, the poor nations are left with less. Yet they have much greater need for oil—for growing food, not for wasting a great deal of it on extravagant cravings.

Fourth, while waiting for a new, clean, and abundant source of energy to be harnessed, people everywhere should stop overheating, overcooling, overlighting, and overspeeding. That would conserve mainly energy but also economize on matter. The surest way is to reject many blessings of technological so-called progress. It is this progress that just the other day brought us the new Gillette razor which can be wholly tossed away when the blades become dull. One should think also of the matter-energy squandered by the tons and tons of Xeroxed material which each day is tossed into the wastebasket without receiving even a glance.

Fifth, man must eliminate the craving for the "bigger and better," for the two-garage cars and other such ludicrous mammoths, as well as for all absurdly contradictory gadgetry, splendidly exemplified by the golf cart. Perhaps one day technological progress will equip the golf cart with an electronically activated club, or even design a remote control which would enable one to play golf sitting in an armchair at home.

Sixth, we should cure ourselves of fashion, a disease of the mind, as stigmatized by Abbot Fernando Galliani, the famous eighteenth century economist. Fashion must be an ugly thing, as Oscar Wilde wittily remarked, if people seek to change it every spring and fall. We now even have fashion for dogs. Aside from the emptiness of it, fashion is probably the greatest energy squanderer in the developed countries, and even in the not-so-developed ones. Were people to cure themselves of the desire to change the style of their clothes every season, their automobiles every year, and their house furniture every other year, manufacturers would have to take the consequences and substitute durability and repairability for planned obsolescence.

Seventh, we should cure ourselves of another disease, which I have called "the circumdrome of the shaving machine." We want to shave more quickly so as to have more time to spend devising a still-faster shaving machine, so that we may spend more time on another, still-faster shaving machine, and so on in an endless, empty progress. Because of this disease, one does not have time to feel that one lives, perhaps not even that one dies. What Alexis de Tocqueville said in 1835 about Americans applies now to many other nations, especially to those at the top of the ladder of wealth.

> If his private affairs leave him any leisure, he instantly plunges into the vortex of politics; and if at the end of a year of unremitting labor he finds he has a few days' vacation, his eager curiosity whirls him over the vast extent of the United States, and he will travel fifteen hundred miles in a few days to shake off his happiness [so that] complete felicity . . . forever escapes him.[43]

This is only a minimal program. But even a complete program could not claim that, if accepted by us all, it would bring about the New Jerusalem. Man will have to struggle with nature in order to maintain his endosomatic existence, and this struggle will continue to have its ramifications in social conflict and possibly also in international conflagrations. The only hope science has is to attenuate these conflicts, not to do away with them, and not by prescriptions of a purely technical or economic nature, but with the aid of a realistic scale of values. One fundamental difference between the human and the other species is that man's actions are guided by his scale of values, because man alone is fully conscious of his existence.

Mankind once received a great message aimed at changing the scale of values of that time: "Thou shalt not kill." Later, he was taught: "Love thy neighbor as thyself." Not all people, but an overwhelming majority have obeyed them; as a result, our common sharing of these terrestrial abodes has become more tranquil than it might have been otherwise.

A commandment befitting our times, in which the struggle of man over natural resources menaces the very survival of the whole species, is:

Love thy species as thyself

so that the present as well as the future generation may enjoy life in a fuller sense.

No legislative body could possibly enforce it, any more than the old commandments could have been so enforced. Values can be changed, if at all, by persuasion, not by coercion. Take a look around the world to convince yourself of this truth.

NOTES

1. J.B.S. Haldane, *The Causes of Evolution* (New York: Harper, 1935), p. 153.

2. Alfred J. Lotka, "The Law of Evolution as a Maximal Principle," *Human Biology* 17 (1945): 188.

3. *Principles of Economics* (8th ed.; New York: Macmillan, 1949), p. xiv.

4. Nicholas Georgescu-Roegen, *The Entropy Law and the Economic Process* (Cambridge, Mass.: Harvard University Press, 1971), p. 56.

5. Joseph Schumpeter, *The Theory of Economic Development* (Cambridge, Mass.: Harvard University Press, 1934), p. 64.

   To show how truly biological Schumpeter's view of the economic process was, I need only mention his insistence that small changes, because they are reversible, do not constitute innovations. This very point appeared in biology only thirty years later with R. Goldschmidt's thesis that evolution requires the emergence of "a successful monster." Certainly, the first railway engine was a successful monster in comparison with its predecessors—the mail coaches. (Nicholas Georgescu-Roegen, *Energy and Economic Myths: Institutional and Analytical Economic Essays* [New York: Pergamon, 1976], chap. 9.)

6. Adam Smith, *The Wealth of Nations*, ed. by E. Cannan (New York: Random House, 1937), pp. 314-15.

7. As documents are concerned, this preoccupation appears for the first time in the Old Testament, where it is provided that every fiftieth year, the Jubilee year, serfs be manumitted, debts forgiven, and other movable things (such as cattle) redistributed. City houses, however, were not involved in the Jubilee redistribution. (Leviticus 25: 8-55.) It goes without saying that a welfare measure of this sort could work only in a half-agricultural, half-pastoral society.

8. Nicholas Georgescu-Roegen, *The Entropy Law and the Economic Process*, pp. 308-11, 348-49.

9. I must hasten to add that the above agrument in no way implies that *Homo Indicus*, as an individual, is not capable of being trained to perform the same tasks as *Homo Americanus*. The argument is concerned, not with the biological individual differences, but with the exosomatic life of each society.

10. See " 'Peace Army' Urged to Aid the Poor," *Honolulu Bulletin*, Mar. 2, 1965, a statement to the press made by the author during the Agricultural Development Council Seminar on Subsistence Agriculture; see also my *Entropy Law and the Economic Process*, p. 364. Of course, there also is the AID Army. But its members are "usually too busy planning and partying . . . to visit the villagers in their mud huts," as reported by Jack Anderson in his column, "U. S. AID Officials Live a Swell Life in Haiti," Aug. 5, 1976.

11. One should not be misled on this point. The land which appears in the conventional production functions is Ricardian land, i.e., mere space. To be sure, Ricardian land is a valid factor of production, but of a nature distinct from that of natural resources. (See my *The Entropy Law* . . . , p. 232, and *Energy and Economic Myths*, chaps. 4, 5.)

12. Georgescu-Roegen, *Analytical Economics: Issues and Problems* (Cambridge, Mass.: Harvard University Press, 1966), pp. 18-19; *The Entropy Law* . . . , pp. 39-42; and *Energy and Economic Myths* . . . , chaps. 1, 3.

13. Georgescu-Roegen, *Analytical Economics* . . . , p. 92; *The Entropy Law* . . . , pp. 3, 276; *Energy and Economic Myths* . . . , chap. 1.

14. The above observations reveal why the Entropy Law is at times stated as "order continuously turns over into disorder."

15. Georgescu-Roegen, *Energy and Economic Myths*. . . , chap. 1, p. 7.

16. Georgescu-Roegen, *The Entropy Law* . . . , pp. 12, 194.

17. Georgescu-Roegen, *Analytical Economics* . . . , p. 94; *The Entropy Law* . . . , p. 278.

18. Georgescu-Roegen, "The Steady State and Ecological Salvation: A Thermodynamic Analysis," *BioScience* (1976) anniversary issue.

19. Kenneth E. Boulding, "The Economics of the Coming Spaceship Earth," in *Toward a Steady-State Economy,* ed. by Herman E. Daly (San Francisco: W. H. Freeman, 1973), pp. 127-32.

20. Georgescu-Roegen, *The Entropy Law* . . . , pp. 224-34.

21. Two qualifications must accompany these statements, irrelevant though they are for the present argument. First, one must also consider the nuclear decay (say, of radium into lead), which diminishes the mass and increases the energy. The second factor is the meteorite fall and any material particles that may escape the earth's gravitation. The meteorite fall, although relatively substantial—50,000 tons per year—comes mainly as useless dust and, hence, may be safely ignored economically.

22. Georgescu-Roegen, "The Steady State and Ecological Salvation."

23. Some symptoms of the pressure of matter may be already detected in the high and rising costs of the installations intended to save on fossil fuels. The solar installation at an elementary school in Atlanta cost almost $1 million, although it provides only 60 percent of the needed energy. A windmill that has a capacity of only a few kilowatts requires tons of aluminum in addition to other materials. Harnessing solar energy in a way other than that provided by natural processes might run aground because of the scarcity of matter. Further, no one can say how a thermonuclear plant will look, if it is ever achieved; but one may note that the accelerator at Fermilab has a diameter of two kilometers (1.25 miles) and involves several thousand magnets.

24. See his "In Defense of a Steady-State Economy," *American Journal of Agricultural Economics* 54 (1972): 945-54.

25. One qualification: even though solar energy always ends up as dissipated thermal energy, it matters for the vegetation and the climate if it is used in a place other than where it has been collected.

26. See Note 23 above.

27. Alvin Weinberg and R. Philip Hammond, "Limits to the Use of Energy," *American Scientist*, July-Aug. 1970, pp. 412-18.

28. Ten years ago, Edward Teller militated against even touching fission reactors because, he thought, the thermonuclear reactor was at hand ("Energy Pattern of the Future," in *Energy and Man: A Symposium*, ed. by Courtney C. Brown [New York: Appleton-Century-Crofts, 1960], pp. 52-72.

29. "The Steady State and Ecological Salvation. . . . "

30. There are other sources not directly connected with solar energy--the energy of the tides, geothermal energy, and, with some great reservation, that of the thermal gradient of the oceans. But while these sources are of great help where they can be used, they are of no importance on a world scale.

31. Georgescu-Roegen, *Energy and Economic Myths*. . . , chap. 1.

32. In his *Energy and Society* (New York: McGraw-Hill, 1955).

33. Georgescu-Roegen, *The Entropy Law* . . . , pp. 17, 278, 283.

34. See Georgescu-Roegen, *Analytical Economics* . . . , p. 960.

35. Georgescu-Roegen, *Energy and Economic Myths* . . . , chap. 1.

36. Georgescu-Roegen, *The Entropy Law* . . . , pp. 19, 301-2; and *Energy and Economic Myths* . . . , chaps. 1, 3.

37. The point leaves out the aggravating fact of the decreasing returns of high-yield varieties with respect to most inputs.

38. Prices are parochial economic coordinates, whatever we may do. They depend upon many things—the income distribution, the distribution of resources, and fashion as well.

39. Georgescu-Roegen, *The Entropy Law*. . . , pp. 21, 304; *Energy and Economic Myths* . . . , chaps. 1, 3.

40. National Research Council, National Academy of Sciences, *Decision Making for Regulating Chemicals in the Environment* (Washington, D.C.: By the Academy, 1975).

41. *Energy and Economic Myths* . . . , chap. 1.

42. The decrease should not be too rapid because the age pyramid would become even more abnormal than it is now. With an exceptionally large proportion of old people in comparison to the working population, we may expect the conflict between the two generations to acquire extreme forms—such as legalized euthanasia.

43. *Democracy in America*, ed. by J. P. Mayer and Max Lerner (New York: Harper & Row, 1966), pp. 508-9.

References

Boulding, Kenneth E. "The Economics of the Coming Spaceship Earth." Reprinted in *Toward a Steady-State Economy*, edited by Herman E. Daly. San Francisco: W. H. Freeman, 1973, pp. 127-32.

Cottrell, Fred. *Energy and Society*. New York: McGraw-Hill, 1955.

Daly, Herman E. "In Defense of a Steady-State Economy." *American Journal of Agricultural Economics* 54 (1972): 945-54.

Georgescu-Roegen, Nicholas. *Analytical Economics: Issues and Problems*. Cambridge, Mass.: Harvard University Press, 1966.

——. *The Entropy Law and the Economic Process*. Cambridge, Mass.: Harvard University Press, 1971.

——. *Energy and Economic Myths: Institutional and Analytical Economic Essays*. New York: Pergamon Press, 1976.

——. "The Steady State and Ecological Salvation: A Thermodynamic Analysis." Anniversary issue of *BioScience* (1976).

Haldane, J. B. S. *The Causes of Evolution*. New York: Harper, 1935.

Lotka, Alfred J. "The Law of Evolution as a Maximal Principle." *Human Biology* 17 (1945).

Marshall, Alfred. *Principles of Economics*. 8th ed. New York: Macmillan, 1949.

National Research Council, National Academy of Sciences, *Decision Making for Regulating Chemicals in the Environment*. Washington, D.C.: By the Academy, 1975.

Schumpeter, Joseph A. *The Theory of Economic Development*. Cambridge, Mass.: Harvard University Press, 1934.

Smith, Adam. *The Wealth of Nations*. Edited by E. Cannan. New York: Random House, 1937.

Teller, Edward. "Energy Pattern of the Future." In *Energy and Man: A Symposium*, edited by Courntney C. Brown. New York: Appleton-Century-Crofts, 1960, pp. 55-72.

de Tocqueville, Alexis. *Democracy in America.* Edited by J. P. Mayer and Max Lerner. New York: Harper, 1966.

Weinberg, Alvin, and Hammond, R. Philip. "Limits to the Use of Energy." *American Scientist*, July-Aug. 1970, pp. 412-18.

PREVIOUS VOLUMES IN THIS SERIES

The Future of Economic Policy, Myron H. Ross, Editor, 1966
Michigan Business Papers, No. 44, 1967

Paul W. McCracken	*The Political Position of the Council of Economic Advisers*
Robert Eisner	*Fiscal and Monetary Policy for Economic Growth*
Theodore W. Schultz	*Public Approaches to Minimize Poverty*
Jesse W. Markham	*Antitrust Policy after a Decade of Vigor*
Kenneth E. Boulding	*The Price System and the Price of the Great Society*
Robert Triffin	*International Monetary Reform*

Key Factors in Economic Growth, Raymond E. Zelder, Editor, 1967
Michigan Business Papers, No. 48, 1968

Martin Bronfenbrenner	*Japanese Economic Development in the Meiji Era, 1867-1912*
Nicholas Spulber	*Is the U.S.S.R. Going Capitalist?*
Milos Samardzija	*Economic Growth and Workers' Management in Yugoslavia*
Lauchlin Currie	*The Crisis in Latin American Development*
Edmundo Flores	*The Alliance for Progress and the Mexican Revolution*
Alexander Eckstein	*The Economic Development of Communist China*

The Cost of Conflict, John A. Copps, Editor, 1968
Michigan Business Papers, No. 51, 1969

Kenneth E. Boulding	*The Threat System*
Thomas C. Schelling	*The Diplomacy of Violence*
Seymour Melman	*The Price of Peace*
Murray L. Weidenbaum	*Towards a Peacetime Economy*
Roger E. Bolton	*National Defense and Regional Development*
Emile Benoit	*Economic Adjustments to Peace in the Far East and to Ending the Arms Race*

America's Cities, Wayland D. Gardner, Editor, 1969
Michigan Business Papers, No. 54, 1970

Wilbur R. Thompson	*The Process of Metropolitan Development: American Experience*
Hugh O. Nourse	*Industrial Location and Land Use in Metropolitan Areas*
Richard F. Muth	*The Economics of Slum Housing*
Dick Netzer	*Urban Government Finance and Urban Development*
Werner Z. Hirsch	*The Urban Challenge to Governments*

Antitrust Policy and Economic Welfare, Werner Sichel, Editor, 1970
Michigan Business Papers, No. 56, 1970

Walter Adams	*The Case for a Comprehensive and Vigorous Antitrust Policy*
Jules Backman	*Holding the Reins on the Trust Busters*
Almarin Phillips	*Antitrust Policies: Could They Be Tools of the Establishment?*
Richard B. Heflebower	*The Conglomerate in American Industry: A Special Antitrust Wrinkle*
Jesse W. Markham	*Structure versus Conduct Criteria in Antitrust*
William G. Shepherd	*Changing Contrasts in British and American Antitrust Policies*

Economic Policies in the 1970s, Alfred K. Ho, Editor, 1971
Michigan Business Papers, No. 57, 1971

James M. Buchanan	*Economists, the Government, and the Economy*
Martin Bronfenbrenner	*Nixonomics and Stagflation Reconsidered*
David I. Fand	*Some Observations on Current Stabilization Policy*
Gardner Ackley	*International Inflation*
Harry G. Johnson	*Inflation: A "Monetarist" View*
Bela Balassa	*Prospects and Problems of British Entry into the Common Market*

The Economics of Environmental Problems, Frank C. Emerson, Editor, 1972
Michigan Business Papers, No. 58, 1973

Joseph L. Fisher	*An Introduction to Environmental Economics*
Lester B. Lave	*The Economic Costs of Air Pollution*
Robert H. Haveman	*The Political Economy of Federal Water Quality Policy*
William S. Vickery	*The Economics of Congestion Control in Urban Transportation*
Jerome Rothenberg	*The Evaluation of Alternative Public Policy Approaches to Environmental Control*